FOODI SMARTLID
COOKBOOK FOR BEGINNERS

Crispy, Easy, Healthy, Fast & Fresh Recipes for Your Pressure Cooker And Air Fryer SmartLid

LINDA COOK

Copyright

No part of this publication may be reproduced, stored in a retrieval system or transmitted in any form or by any means, electronic, mechanical, photocopying, recording, scanning or otherwise, except as permitted under Sections 107 or 108 of the 1976 United States Copyright Act, without the prior written permission of the Publisher. Requests to the Publisher for permission should be addressed to the Permissions Department.

Limit of Liability/Disclaimer of Warranty: The Publisher and the author make no representations or warranties with respect to the accuracy or completeness of the contents of this work and specifically disclaim all warranties, including without limitation warranties of fitness for a particular purpose. No warranty may be created or extended by sales or promotional materials. The advice and strategies contained herein may not be suitable for every situation. This work is sold with the understanding that the publisher is not engaged in rendering medical, legal or other professional advice or services.

If professional assistance is required, the services of a competent professional person should be sought. Neither the Publisher nor the author shall be liable for damages arising here from. The fact that an individual, organization or website is referred to in this work as a citation and/or potential source of further information does not mean that the author or the Publisher endorses the information the individual, organization or website may provide or recommendations they/it may make. Further, readers should be aware that Internet websites listed in this work might have changed or disappeared between when this work was written and when it is read.
The author publishes its books in a variety of electronic and print formats. Some content that appears in print may not be available in electronic books, and vice versa.

TRADEMARKS: All other trademarks are the property of their respective owners. The author is not associated with any product or vendor mentioned in this book.

Table of Contents

Table of Contents	**4**
INTRODUCTION	**9**
How Does the Foodi SmartLid Works?	9
Benefits of the Foodi SmartLid	10
Vegetables Recipes	**11**
Air Fryer Asparagus	11
Crispy Ratatouille	11
Avocado Fries	12
Warm Quinoa And Potato Salad	13
Parmesan Breaded Zucchini Chips	14
Bell Pepper-Corn Wrapped in Tortilla	15
Baked Cheesy Eggplant with Marinara	15
Spicy Sweet Potato Fries	16
Creamy Spinach Quiche	17
Cauliflower Rice	18
Buttery Carrots With Pancetta	18
Stuffed Mushrooms	19
Air Fried Carrots, Yellow Squash & Zucchini	20
Winter Vegetarian Frittata	20
Braised Red Cabbage With Apples	21
Air Fried Kale Chips	22
Zucchini Omelet	22
Cheesy Cauliflower Fritters	23
Cauliflower Bites	23
Buttered Carrot-Zucchini with Mayo	24
Sage-Butter Spaghetti Squash	24
Roasted Vegetables Salad	25
Cheddar, Squash, And Zucchini Casserole	26
Zucchini Parmesan Chips	27
Jalapeño Cheese Balls	27
Crispy Roasted Broccoli	28
Creamy And Cheese Broccoli Bake	29
Coconut Battered Cauliflower Bites	29
Crispy Jalapeno Coins	30
Buffalo Cauliflower	31
Crisped Baked Cheese Stuffed Chile Pepper	31
Jicama Fries	32
Jumbo Stuffed Mushrooms	32
Air Fryer Brussels Sprouts	33
Spaghetti Squash Tots	33
Crispy And Healthy Avocado Fingers	34
Onion Rings	34
Cinnamon Butternut Squash Fries	35
Poultry Recipes	**36**
Korean Chicken Wings	36
Enchilada-Braised Chicken Breasts	37
Sweet And Sour Chicken	38
Perfect Chicken Parmesan	38
Basil-Garlic Breaded Chicken Bake	39
Honey-Chipotle Chicken Wings	39
Buffalo Chicken Wings	40
Honey and Wine Chicken Breasts	41
Chicken Fajitas	41
Crispy Honey Garlic Chicken Wings	42
Zingy & Nutty Chicken Wings	42
Chicken Fillets, Brie & Ham	42

Ricotta and Parsley Stuffed Turkey Breasts	43	Keto Parmesan Crusted Pork Chops	62
Chicken-Fried Steak Supreme	43	Pork Wonton Wonderful	62
Cheesy Chicken Tenders	44	Tuscan Pork Chops	63
Lemon-Pepper Chicken Wings	45	Pork Loin With Apples	64
Easy Turkey Breast	46	Crispy Breaded Pork Chops	65
Caesar Marinated Grilled Chicken	46	Crispy Roast Garlic-Salt Pork	65
Minty Chicken-Fried Pork Chops	47	Peanut Satay Pork	66
Crispy Southern Fried Chicken	48	Pork Tenderloin And Coconut Rice	66
Chicken Roast with Pineapple Salsa	48	Ginger, Garlic	67
Tex-Mex Turkey Burgers	49	And Pork Dumplings	67
Air Fryer Turkey Breast	49	Pork Tenderloin with Braised Apples	67
Cheese Stuffed Chicken	50	Caramelized Pork Shoulder	69
Orange Curried Chicken Stir-Fry	50	Curry Pork Roast in Coconut Sauce	70
Mustard Chicken Tenders	51	Chinese Salt and Pepper Pork Chop Stir-fry	70
Chicken Pot Pie with Coconut Milk	51	Roasted Pork Tenderloin	71
Chicken Nuggets	51	Garlic Putter Pork Chops	72
Cheesy Chicken Fritters	52	Fried Pork with Sweet and Sour Glaze	72
Chicken BBQ with Sweet And Sour Sauce	52	Pork Cutlet Rolls	73
Crusted Chicken Tenders	53	Oregano-Paprika on Breaded Pork	73
Air Fryer Chicken Parmesan	54	Bacon Wrapped Pork Tenderloin	74
Chicken BBQ Recipe from Peru	54	Dijon Garlic Pork Tenderloin	74
Ricotta and Parsley Stuffed Turkey Breasts	55	Pork Neck with Salad	75
Cheesy Turkey-Rice with Broccoli	55	Cajun Pork Steaks	75
Jerk Chicken Wings	56	Wonton Taco Cups	76

Pork Recipes 57

		Cajun Sweet-Sour Grilled Pork	76
Pork Shoulder Chops With Soy Sauce, Maple Syrup, And Carrots	57	Chinese Braised Pork Belly	77
		Air Fryer Sweet and Sour Pork	77
Panko-Breaded Pork Chops	58	Pork Loin with Potatoes	77
Apricot Glazed Pork Tenderloins	58	Fried Pork Scotch Egg	78
Pulled Pork	59	Roasted Char Siew (Pork Butt)	79
Barbecue Flavored Pork Ribs	60	Juicy Pork Ribs Ole	80
Rustic Pork Ribs	60	Asian Pork Chops	80
Fried Pork Quesadilla	61	Teriyaki Pork Rolls	81

Ham and Cheese Rollups	81
Vietnamese Pork Chops	82

Beef Recipes 83

Cheeseburger Egg Rolls	83
Brisket With Veggies	84
Juicy Cheeseburgers	85
Country Fried Steak	85
Spicy Thai Beef Stir-Fry	87
Lamb Casserole	87
Barbecued Baby Back Ribs	88
Sausage And Peppers	89
Spicy Sausage And Chard Pasta Sauce	90
Meat Lovers' Pizza	91
Chimichurri Skirt Steak	92
Ground Beef Stew	93
Creamy Burger & Potato Bake	94
Lamb with Mexican Sauce	94
Beefy And Cheesy Spanish Rice Casserole	95
Pulled BBQ Beef Sandwiches	96
Beef & veggie Spring Rolls	97
Lamb And Eggplant Pasta Casserole	98
Beef Stroganoff	99
Lamb Shanks Provençal	99
Beefy Steak Topped with Chimichurri Sauce	100
Beef Ribeye Steak	101
Air fryer Roast Beef	101
Beef Korma	102
Cumin-Paprika Rubbed Beef Brisket	102
Lamb Shanks With Pancetta	103
Sugar-And-Spice Beef Empanadas	104
Crispy Mongolian Beef	105
Beef & Lemon Schnitzel for One	105
Crispy Beef Schnitzel	106

Simple Steak	106
Garlic-Cumin And Orange Juice Marinated Steak	107
Beef Taco Fried Egg Rolls	107
Beef With Beans	107
Swedish Meatballs	108
Rice and Meatball Stuffed Bell Peppers	109
Pub Style Corned Beef Egg Rolls	109
Stir-Fried Steak and Cabbage	110
Reuben Egg Rolls	111
Air-Fried Philly Cheesesteak	111
Herbed Roast Beef	112
Tender Beef with Sour Cream Sauce	113
Beef Empanadas	113
Beef Pot Pie	114
Bolognaise Sauce	115
Breaded Spam Steaks	115
Air Fryer Burgers	116
Cheese-Stuffed Meatballs	116
Roasted Stuffed Peppers	117
Air Fried Steak Sandwich	117
Carrot and Beef Cocktail Balls	118
Beef Steaks with Beans	119
Air Fryer Beef Steak	119
Mushroom Meatloaf	120
Beef and Broccoli	120
Air Fryer Beef Fajitas	121

Seafood Recipes 122

Coconut Shrimp	122
Bacon Wrapped Shrimp	122
Shrimp And Tomatillo Casserole	123
Grilled Salmon	124
Air Fryer Salmon	124

Beer Potato Fish	125
Steamed Salmon & Sauce	125
Sweet And Savory Breaded Shrimp	126
Indian Fish Fingers	127
Healthy Fish and Chips	127
Quick Paella	128
Coconut Shrimp	128
3-Ingredient Air Fryer Catfish	129
Tuna Veggie Stir-Fry	129
Salmon Quiche	130
Cilantro-Lime Fried Shrimp	130
Lemony Tuna	131
Bang Bang Panko Breaded Fried Shrimp	132
Grilled Soy Salmon Fillets	132
Flying Fish	133
Pistachio-Crusted Lemon-Garlic Salmon	133
Louisiana Shrimp Po Boy	134
Old Bay Crab Cakes	135
Scallops and Spring Veggies	136
Air Fryer Salmon Patties	136
Salmon Noodles	137
Beer-Battered Fish and Chips	137
Tuna Stuffed Potatoes	138
Fried Calamari	138
Soy and Ginger Shrimp	139
Crispy Cheesy Fish Fingers	139
Panko-Crusted Tilapia	140
Potato Crusted Salmon	141
Salmon Croquettes	141
Snapper Scampi	142
Tha Fish Cakes With Mango Relish	142
Air Fryer Fish Tacos	143
Firecracker Shrimp	143
Sesame Seeds Coated Fish	144
Bacon Wrapped Scallops	145
Crispy Paprika Fish Fillets	145
Parmesan Shrimp	146
Flaky Fish Quesadilla	146
Quick Fried Catfish	147
Honey Glazed Salmon	148
Fish and Chips	148
Fish Sandwiches	149
Crab Cakes	149
Crispy Air Fried Sushi Roll	150

Sweet Recipes — 151

Perfect Cinnamon Toast	151
Easy Baked Chocolate Mug Cake	151
Angel Food Cake	152
Fried Peaches	152
Easy Donuts	153
Apple Pie in Air Fryer	153
Raspberry Cream Rol-Ups	153
Air Fryer Chocolate Cake	155
Banana-Choco Brownies	155
Chocolate Donuts	156
Easy Air fryer Donuts	156
Cinnamon Rolls	157
Fried Bananas with Chocolate Sauce	157
Apple Hand Pies	158
Chocolaty Banana Muffins	158
Blueberry Lemon Muffins	159
Sweet Cream Cheese Wontons	159
Air Fryer Cinnamon Rolls	160
Bread Pudding with Cranberry	160
Black and White Brownies	161
French Toast Bites	161

Baked Apple	*162*
Coffee And Blueberry Cake	*162*
Cinnamon Sugar	*163*
Roasted Chickpeas	*163*
Cherry-Choco Bars	*163*
Cinnamon Fried Bananas	*164*
Coconutty Lemon Bars	*164*
Conclusions	**165**
About the Author	**166**

INTRODUCTION

The Foodi SmartLid is revolutionary! It transforms your pressure cooker foods into crispy ones. It also works as a stand-alone air-fryer by roasting, baking, crisping, dehydrating, and air frying any food inside.

With this Foodi SmartLid cookbook, there's much to savor. Move Over French Fries—Cook your favorites, indulge in guilty pleasures, and discover new delights you'd never thought to pressure cook and air fry.

The Foodi SmartLid is a fantastic way to cook food that is healthy and easy. It is a fast and safe way of cooking, provides a healthy option, and is easy to clean once it has been used.

Who knew one cooking appliance could do so much so deliciously well? This Foodi SmartLid Cookbook knows—and now you do, too.

Using the Foodi SmartLid is an easy way to cook delicious healthy meals. Rather than cooking the food in oil and hot fat that may affect your health, the machine uses rapid hot air to circulate around and cook meals. This allows the outside of your food to be crispy and also makes sure that the inside layers are cooked through.

The Foodi SmartLid allows us to cook almost everything and a lot of dishes. We can use the Foodi SmartLid for cooking Meat, vegetables, poultry, fruit, fish, and a wide variety of desserts. It is possible to prepare your entire meals, starting from appetizers to main courses as well as desserts. Not to mention, Foodi SmartLid also allows homemade preserves or even delicious sweets and cakes.

How Does the Foodi SmartLid Works?

This Innovative instant air fryer crisp pot technology ensures tender, juicy meals with a crisp, golden finish — every time.

The technology of the Foodi SmartLid is very simple. Fried foods get their crunchy texture because hot oil heats foods quickly and evenly on their surface. Oil is an excellent heat conductor, which helps with fast and simultaneous cooking across all of the ingredients. For decades cooks have used convection ovens to try to mimic the effects of frying or to cook the whole surface of the food. But the air never circulates quickly enough to achieve that delicious surface crisp we all love in fried foods.

With this mechanism, the air is circulated on high degrees, up to 200° C, to "air fry" any food such as fish, chicken or chips, etc. This technology has changed the whole idea of cooking by reducing the fat up to 80% compared to old-fashioned deep fat frying.

The Foodi SmartLid cooking releases the heat through a heating element that cooks the food in a healthier and more appropriate way. There's also an exhaust fan right above the cooking chamber, which provides the food required airflow. This way, food is cooked with constant heated air. This leads to the same heating temperature reaching every single part of the food that is being cooked. So, this is only grill and the exhaust fan that is helping the Foodi SmartLid to boost air at a constantly high speed in order to cook healthy food with less fat.

The internal pressure increases the temperature that will then be controlled by the exhaust system. Exhaust fan also releases extra filtered air to cook the food in a much healthier way. The Foodi SmartLid has no odor at all, and it is absolutely harmless, making it user and environment-friendly.

Benefits of the Foodi SmartLid

The amazing benefits include:

- Healthier, oil-free meals
- It eliminates cooking odors through internal air filters
- Makes cleaning easier due to lack of oil grease
- Foodi SmartLid is able to bake, grill, roast and fry providing more options
- A safer method of cooking compared to deep frying with exposed hot oil
- Has the ability to set and leave as most models and it includes a digital timer

The Foodi SmartLid is an all-in-one that allows cooking to be easy and quick. It also leads to a lot of possibilities once you get to know it. Once you learn the basics and become familiar with your Foodi SmartLid, you can feel free to experiment and modify the recipes in the way you prefer. You can prepare a wide number of dishes with the Foodi SmartLid, and you can adapt your favorite stove-top dish, so it becomes Air Fryer–friendly. It all boils down to variety and lots of options, right?
Cooking perfect and delicious as well as healthy meals has never been easier. You can see how this recipe collection proves itself.

Enjoy!

Vegetables Recipes

Air Fryer Asparagus

PREP: 5 MINUTES • COOK TIME: 8 MINUTES • TOTAL: 13 MINUTES
SERVES: 2

Ingredients
Nutritional yeast
Olive oil non-stick spray
One bunch of asparagus

Directions

1. **Preparing the Ingredients.** Wash asparagus and then trim off thick, woody ends.
Spray asparagus with olive oil spray and sprinkle with yeast.
2. **Air Frying.** In your Foodi SmartLid, lay asparagus in a singular layer. Set the temperature to 360°F, and set time to 8 minutes.

PER SERVING: CALORIES: 17; FAT: 4G; PROTEIN: 9G

Crispy Ratatouille

PREP: 5 MINUTES • PRESSURE: 4 MINUTES • BROIL: 5 MINUTES • TOTAL: 14 MINUTES • PRESSURE LEVEL: HIGH • RELEASE: QUICK
SERVES 4

Ingredients
Kosher salt, for salting and seasoning
1 small eggplant, peeled and sliced ½ inch thick
1 medium zucchini, sliced ½ inch thick
2 tablespoons olive oil
1 cup chopped onion
3 garlic cloves, minced or pressed
1 small green bell pepper, cut into ½-inch chunks (about 1 cup)
1 small red bell pepper, cut into ½-inch chunks (about 1 cup)
1 rib celery, sliced (about 1 cup)
1 (14.5-ounce) can diced tomatoes, undrained
¼ cup water
½ teaspoon dried oregano
¼ teaspoon freshly ground black pepper
2 tablespoons minced fresh basil
¼ cup pitted green or black olives (optional)

Directions

1. **Preparing the Ingredients**. Place a rack on a baking sheet. With kosher salt, very liberally salt one side of the eggplant and zucchini slices, and place them, salted-side down, on the rack. Salt the other side. Let the slices sit for 15 to 20 minutes, or until they start to exude water (you'll see it beading up on the surface of the slices and dripping into the sheet pan). Rinse the

slices, and blot them dry. Cut the zucchini slices into quarters and the eggplant slices into eighths.

Turn the Foodi SmartLid to "Sauté", heat the olive oil until it shimmers and flows like water. Add the onion and garlic, and sprinkle with a pinch or two of kosher salt. Cook for about 3 minutes, stirring until the onions just begin to brown.

Add the eggplant, zucchini, green bell pepper, red bell pepper, celery, and tomatoes with their juice, water, and oregano.

2. **High pressure for 4 minutes**. Lock the pressure cooking lid on the Foodi SmartLid and then cook for 4 minutes. To get 4-minutes cook time, press "Pressure" button and use the Time Adjustment button to adjust the cook time to 4 minutes.
3. **Pressure Release**. Use the quick-release method.
4. **Finish the dish**. Unlock and remove the lid. Close the Air Fryer Lid, select BROIL, and set the time to 5 minutes. Select START to begin. Cook until top is browned.

Stir in the pepper, basil, and olives (if using). Taste, adjust the seasoning as needed, and serve.

While this vegetable dish is usually served on its own, it's great tossed with cooked pasta or served over polenta.

PER SERVING: CALORIES: 149; FAT: 8G; SODIUM: 55MG; CARBOHYDRATES: 20G; FIBER: 8G; PROTEIN: 4G

Avocado Fries
PREP: 10 MINUTES • COOK TIME: 7 MINUTES • TOTAL: 17 MINUTES
SERVES: 6

Ingredients
1 avocado
½ tsp. salt
½ C. panko breadcrumbs
Bean liquid (aquafaba) from a 15-ounce can of white or garbanzo beans

Directions:
Preparing the Ingredients. Peel, pit, and slice up avocado.

Toss salt and breadcrumbs together in a bowl. Place aquafaba into another bowl.

Dredge slices of avocado first in aquafaba and then in panko, making sure you get an even coating.

Air Frying. Place coated avocado slices into a single layer in the Foodi SmartLid. Set temperature to 390°F, and set time to 5 minutes.

Serve with your favorite keto dipping sauce!

PER SERVING: CALORIES: 102; FAT: 22G; PROTEIN:9G; SUGAR:1G

Warm Quinoa And Potato Salad

PREP: 5 MINUTES • PRESSURE: 10 MINUTES • BROIL: 5 MINUTES • TOTAL: 20 MINUTES • PRESSURE LEVEL: HIGH • RELEASE: QUICK
SERVES 6

Ingredients

¼ cup white balsamic vinegar
1 tablespoon Dijon mustard
1 teaspoon sweet paprika
½ teaspoon ground black pepper
¼ teaspoon celery seeds
¼ teaspoon salt
¼ cup olive oil
1½ pounds tiny white potatoes, halved
1 cup blond (white) quinoa
1 medium shallot, minced
2 medium celery stalks, thinly sliced
1 large dill pickle, diced

Directions

1. **Preparing the Ingredients.** Whisk the vinegar, mustard, paprika, pepper, celery seeds, and salt in a large serving bowl until smooth; whisk in the olive oil in a thin, steady stream until the dressing is fairly creamy.

   Place the potatoes and quinoa in the Foodi SmartLid ; add enough cold tap water so that the ingredients are submerged by 3 inches (some of the quinoa may float).

2. **High pressure for 10 minutes.** Lock the pressure cooking lid on the Foodi SmartLid and then cook for 10 minutes. To get 10-minutes cook time, press "Pressure" button and use the Time Adjustment button to adjust the cook time to 10 minutes.

3. **Pressure Release.** Use the quick-release method to bring the pot's pressure back to normal.

4. **Finish the dish.** Unlock and open the pot. Close the Air Fryer Lid. Select BROIL, and set the time to 5 minutes. Select START to begin. Cook until top is browned. Drain the contents of the pot into a colander lined with paper towels or into a fine-mesh sieve in the sink. Do not rinse.

   Transfer the potatoes and quinoa to the large bowl with the dressing. Add the shallot, celery, and pickle; toss gently and set aside for a minute or two to warm up the vegetables.

PER SERVING: CALORIES: 244; FAT: 12G; PROTEIN: 12G; FIBER: 2.4G

Parmesan Breaded Zucchini Chips

PREP: 15 MINUTES • COOK TIME: 20 MINUTES • TOTAL: 35 MINUTES
SERVES: 5

Ingredients

For the zucchini chips:
2 medium zucchini
2 eggs
⅓ cup bread crumbs
⅓ cup grated Parmesan cheese
Salt
Pepper
Cooking oil

For the lemon aioli:
½ cup mayonnaise
½ tablespoon olive oil
Juice of ½ lemon
1 teaspoon minced garlic
Salt
Pepper

Directions

1. **Preparing the Ingredients.** To make the zucchini chips:
   Slice the zucchini into thin chips (about ⅛ inch thick) using a knife or mandoline.
   In a small bowl, beat the eggs. In another small bowl, combine the bread crumbs, Parmesan cheese, and salt and pepper to taste.
   Spray the Foodi SmartLid basket with cooking oil.
   Dip the zucchini slices one at a time in the eggs and then the bread crumb mixture. You can also sprinkle the bread crumbs onto the zucchini slices with a spoon.
   Place the zucchini chips in the Foodi SmartLid basket, but do not stack.
2. **Air Frying.** Lock the air fryer lid. Cook in batches. Spray the chips with cooking oil from a distance (otherwise, the breading may fly off). Cook for 10 minutes.
   Remove the cooked zucchini chips from the Foodi SmartLid, then repeat step 5 with the remaining zucchini.

To make the lemon aioli:
While the zucchini is cooking, combine the mayonnaise, olive oil, lemon juice, and garlic in a small bowl, adding salt and pepper to taste. Mix well until fully combined.
Cool the zucchini and serve alongside the aioli.

PER SERVING: CALORIES: 192; FAT: 13G; PROTEIN: 6G; FIBER: 4G

Bell Pepper-Corn Wrapped in Tortilla

PREP: 5 MINUTES • COOK TIME: 15 MINUTES • TOTAL: 20 MINUTES
SERVES: 4

Ingredients

1 small red bell pepper, chopped
1 small yellow onion, diced
1 tablespoon water
2 cobs grilled corn kernels
4 large tortillas
4 pieces commercial vegan nuggets, chopped
mixed greens for garnish

Directions

1. **Preparing the Ingredients.** Preheat the Foodi SmartLid to 400°F.
   In a skillet heated over medium heat, water sauté the vegan nuggets together with the onions, bell peppers, and corn kernels. Set aside.
   Place filling inside the corn tortillas.
2. **Air Frying.** Lock the air fryer lid. Fold the tortillas and place inside the Foodi SmartLid and cook for 15 minutes until the tortilla wraps are crispy.
   Serve with mix greens on top.

PER SERVING: CALORIES: 548; FAT: 20.7G; PROTEIN: 46G

Baked Cheesy Eggplant with Marinara

PREP: 5 MINUTES • COOK TIME: 45 MINUTES • TOTAL: 50 MINUTES
SERVES: 3

Ingredients

1 clove garlic, sliced
1 large eggplants
1 tablespoon olive oil
1 tablespoon olive oil
1/2 pinch salt, or as needed
1/4 cup and 2 tablespoons dry bread crumbs
1/4 cup and 2 tablespoons ricotta cheese
1/4 cup grated Parmesan cheese
1/4 cup grated Parmesan cheese
1/4 cup water, plus more as needed
1/4 teaspoon red pepper flakes
1-1/2 cups prepared marinara sauce
1-1/2 teaspoons olive oil
2 tablespoons shredded pepper jack cheese
salt and freshly ground black pepper to taste

Directions

1. **Preparing the Ingredients.** Cut eggplant crosswise in 5 pieces. Peel and chop two pieces into ½-inch cubes.
   Lightly grease baking pan of Foodi SmartLid with 1 tbsp olive oil for 5 minutes, heat oil at 390°F. Add half eggplant strips and cook for 2 minutes per side. Transfer to a plate.
   Add 1 ½ tsp olive oil and add garlic. Cook for a minute. Add chopped eggplants. Season with pepper flakes and salt. Cook for 4 minutes. Lower heat to 330°F. and continue cooking eggplants until soft, around 8 minutes more.
   Stir in water and marinara sauce. Cook for 7 minutes until heated through. Stirring every now and then. Transfer to a bowl.

In a bowl, whisk well pepper, salt, pepper jack cheese, Parmesan cheese, and ricotta. Evenly spread cheeses over eggplant strips and then fold in half.

Lay folded eggplant in baking pan. Pour marinara sauce on top.

In a small bowl whisk well olive oil, and bread crumbs. Sprinkle all over sauce.

2. **Air Frying.** Lock the air fryer lid. Cook for 15 minutes at 390°F until tops are lightly browned.

Serve and enjoy.

PER SERVING: CALORIES: 405; FAT: 21.4G; PROTEIN: 12.7G

Spicy Sweet Potato Fries

PREP: 5 MINUTES • COOK TIME: 37 MINUTES • TOTAL: 45 MINUTES
SERVES: 4

Ingredients
2 tbsp. sweet potato fry seasoning mix
2 tbsp. olive oil
2 sweet potatoes

Seasoning Mix:
2 tbsp. salt
1 tbsp. cayenne pepper
1 tbsp. dried oregano
1 tbsp. fennel
2 tbsp. coriander

Directions:

1. **Preparing the Ingredients.** Slice both ends off sweet potatoes and peel. Slice lengthwise in half and again crosswise to make four pieces from each potato.
Slice each potato piece into 2-3 slices, then slice into fries.
Grind together all of seasoning mix ingredients and mix in the salt.
Ensure the Foodi SmartLid is preheated to 350 degrees.
Toss potato pieces in olive oil, sprinkling with seasoning mix and tossing well to coat thoroughly.

2. **Air Frying.** Add fries to Foodi SmartLid basket. Lock the air fryer lid. Set temperature to 350°F, and set time to 27 minutes. Select START to begin.
Take out the basket and turn fries. Turn off Foodi SmartLid and let cook 10-12 minutes till fries are golden.

PER SERVING: CALORIES: 89; FAT: 14G; PROTEIN: 8Gs; SUGAR:3G

Creamy Spinach Quiche

PREP: 10 MINUTES • COOK TIME: 20 MINUTES • TOTAL: 30 MINUTES
SERVES: 4

Ingredients
Premade quiche crust, chilled and rolled flat to a 7-inch round
eggs
¼ cup of milk
Pinch of salt and pepper
1 clove of garlic, peeled and finely minced
½ cup of cooked spinach, drained and coarsely chopped
¼ cup of shredded mozzarella cheese
¼ cup of shredded cheddar cheese

Directions
1. **Preparing the Ingredients.** Preheat the Foodi SmartLid to 360 degrees.
   Press the premade crust into a 7-inch pie tin, or any appropriately sized glass or ceramic heat-safe dish. Press and trim at the edges if necessary. With a fork, pierce several holes in the dough to allow air circulation and prevent cracking of the crust while cooking.
   In a mixing bowl, beat the eggs until fluffy and until the yolks and white are evenly combined.
   Add milk, garlic, spinach, salt and pepper, and half the cheddar and mozzarella cheese to the eggs. Set the rest of the cheese aside for now, and stir the mixture until completely blended. Make sure the spinach is not clumped together, but rather spread among the other ingredients.
   Pour the mixture into the pie crust, slowly and carefully to avoid splashing. The mixture should almost fill the crust, but not completely – leaving a ¼ inch of crust at the edges.
2. **Air Frying.** Lock the air fryer lid. Set the air-fryer timer for 15 minutes. After 15 minutes, the Foodi SmartLid will shut off, and the quiche will already be firm and the crust beginning to brown. Sprinkle the rest of the cheddar and mozzarella cheese on top of the quiche filling. Reset the Foodi SmartLid at 360 degrees for 5 minutes. After 5 minutes, when the Foodi SmartLid shuts off, the cheese will have formed an exquisite crust on top and the quiche will be golden brown and perfect. Remove from the Foodi SmartLid using oven mitts or tongs, and set on a heat-safe surface to cool for a few minutes before cutting.

Cauliflower Rice

PREP: 5 MINUTES • COOK TIME: 20 MINUTES • TOTAL: 25 MINUTES
SERVES: 4

Ingredients
Round 1:
 tsp. turmeric
1 C. diced carrot
½ C. diced onion
2 tbsp. low-sodium soy sauce
½ block of extra firm tofu

Round 2:
½ C. frozen peas
2 minced garlic cloves
½ C. chopped broccoli
1 tbsp. minced ginger
1 tbsp. rice vinegar
1 ½ tsp. toasted sesame oil
2 tbsp. reduced-sodium soy sauce
3 C. riced cauliflower

Directions:
1. **Preparing the Ingredients.** Crumble tofu in a large bowl and toss with all the Round one ingredient.
2. **Air Frying.** Lock the air fryer lid. Preheat the Foodi SmartLid to 370 degrees, set temperature to 370°F, and set time to 10 minutes and cook 10 minutes, making sure to shake once.
   In another bowl, toss ingredients from Round 2 together.
   Add Round 2 mixture to Foodi SmartLid and cook another 10 minutes, ensuring to shake 5 minutes in.
   Enjoy!

PER SERVING: CALORIES: 67; FAT: 8G; PROTEIN: 3G; SUGAR: 0G

Buttery Carrots With Pancetta

PREP: 5 MINUTES • PRESSURE: 7 MINUTES • BROIL: 5 MINUTES • TOTAL: 17 MINUTES • PRESSURE LEVEL: HIGH • RELEASE: QUICK
SERVES 4 - 6

Ingredients
4 ounces pancetta, diced
1 medium leek, white and pale green parts only, sliced lengthwise, washed, and thinly sliced
¼ cup moderately sweet white wine, such as a dry Riesling
1 pound baby carrots
½ teaspoon ground black pepper
2 tablespoons unsalted butter, cut into small bits

Directions
1. **Preparing the Ingredients.** Put the pancetta in the Foodi SmartLid turned to the "Air Fry" function and use the Time Adjustment button to adjust the cook time to 5 minutes. Add the leek; cook, often stirring, until softened. Pour in the wine and scrape up any browned bits at the bottom of the pot as it comes to a simmer.
   Add the carrots and pepper; stir well. Scrape and pour the contents of the Foodi SmartLid into a 1-quart, round, high-sided soufflé or baking dish. Dot with the bits of butter. Lay a piece of parchment paper on top of the dish, then a piece of aluminum foil. Seal the foil tightly over the baking dish.
   Set the Foodi SmartLid rack inside, and pour in 2 cups water. Use aluminum foil to build a sling for the baking dish; lower the baking dish into the cooker.
2. **High pressure for 7 minutes.** Lock the Pressure cooking lid on the Foodi SmartLid and then cook for 7 minutes.

To get 7-minutes cook time, press "Pressure" button and use the Time Adjustment button to adjust the cook time to 7 minutes.
3. **Pressure Release.** Use the quick-release method to return the pot's pressure to normal.
4. **Finish the dish.** Close the Air Fryer Lid. Select BROIL, and set the time to 5 minutes. Select START to begin. Cook until top is browned.

Unlock and open the pot. Use the foil sling to lift the baking dish out of the cooker. Uncover, stir well, and serve.

Stuffed Mushrooms
PREP: 7 MINUTES • COOK TIME: 8 MINUTES • TOTAL: 15 MINUTES
SERVES: 12

Ingredients
2 Rashers Bacon, Diced
½ Onion, Diced
½ Bell Pepper, Diced
1 Small Carrot, Diced
24 Medium Size Mushrooms (Separate the caps & stalks)
1 cup Shredded Cheddar Plus Extra for the Top
½ cup Sour Cream

Directions:
1. **Preparing the Ingredients.** Chop the mushrooms stalks finely and fry them up with the bacon, onion, pepper and carrot at 350 ° for 8 minutes.

When the veggies are fairly tender, stir in the sour cream & the cheese. Keep on the heat until the cheese has melted and everything is mixed nicely.

Now grab the mushroom caps and heap a plop of filling on each one.

Place in the fryer basket and top with a little extra cheese.

Air Fried Carrots, Yellow Squash & Zucchini

PREP: 5 MINUTES • COOK TIME: 35 MINUTES •
TOTAL: 40 MINUTES
SERVES: 4

Ingredients
1 tbsp. chopped tarragon leaves
½ tsp. white pepper
1 tsp. salt
1 pound yellow squash
1 pound zucchini
6 tsp. olive oil
½ pound carrots

Directions:

1. **Preparing the Ingredients.** Stem and root the end of squash and zucchini and cut in ¾-inch half-moons. Peel and cut carrots into 1-inch cubes
Combine carrot cubes with 2 teaspoons of olive oil, tossing to combine.
2. **Air Frying.** Pour into the Foodi SmartLid basket. Lock the air fryer lid. Set temperature to 400°F, and set time to 5 minutes.
As carrots cook, drizzle remaining olive oil over squash and zucchini pieces, then season with pepper and salt. Toss well to coat.
Add squash and zucchini when the timer for carrots goes off. Cook 30 minutes, making sure to toss 2-3 times during the cooking process.
Once done, take out veggies and toss with tarragon. Serve up warm!

PER SERVING: CALORIES: 122; FAT: 9G; PROTEIN: 6G; SUGAR:0G

Winter Vegetarian Frittata

PREP: 5 MINUTES • COOK TIME: 30 MINUTES •
TOTAL: 35 MINUTES
SERVES: 4

Ingredients
1 leek, peeled and thinly sliced into rings
2 cloves garlic, finely minced
3 medium-sized carrots, finely chopped
2 tablespoons olive oil
6 large-sized eggs
Sea salt and ground black pepper, to taste
1/2 teaspoon dried marjoram, finely minced
1/2 cup yellow cheese of choice

Directions:

1. **Preparing the Ingredients.** Sauté the leek, garlic, and carrot in hot olive oil until they are tender and fragrant; reserve.
In the meantime, preheat your Foodi SmartLid to 330 degrees F.
In a bowl, whisk the eggs along with the salt, ground black pepper, and marjoram.
Then, grease the inside of your baking dish with a nonstick cooking spray. Pour the whisked eggs into the baking dish. Stir in the sautéed carrot mixture. Top with the cheese shreds.
2. **Air Frying.** Place the baking dish in the Foodi SmartLid cooking basket. Lock the air fryer lid. Cook about 30 minutes and serve warm.

Braised Red Cabbage With Apples

PREP: 5 MINUTES • PRESSURE: 13 MINUTES • BROIL: 23 MINUTES • TOTAL: 18 MINUTES • PRESSURE LEVEL: HIGH • RELEASE: QUICK
SERVES 4

Ingredients

4 thin bacon slices, chopped
1 small red onion, chopped
1 medium tart green apple, such as Granny Smith, peeled, cored, and chopped
1 teaspoon dried thyme
¼ teaspoon ground allspice
¼ teaspoon ground mace
1 tablespoon packed dark brown sugar
1 tablespoon balsamic vinegar
1 medium red cabbage (about 2 pounds), cored and thinly sliced
½ cup chicken broth

Directions

1. **Preparing the Ingredients**. Lock the air fryer lid. Fry the bacon in the Foodi SmartLid turned to the "Air Fry" function, until crisp, about 4 minutes.
   Add the onion to the pot; cook, often stirring, until soft, about 4 minutes. Add the apple, thyme, allspice, and mace. Cook about 1 minute, stirring all the while, until fragrant. Stir in the brown sugar and vinegar; keep stirring until bubbling, about 1 minute.
   Add the cabbage; toss well to mix evenly with the other ingredients. Drizzle the broth over the cabbage mixture.
2. **High pressure for 13 minutes**. Lock the Pressure cooking Lid on the Foodi SmartLid and then cook for 13 minutes. To get 13-minutes cook time, press "Pressure" button, and use the Time Adjustment button to adjust the cook time to 13 minutes.
3. **Pressure Release**. Use the quick-release method to return the pot to normal pressure.

Unlock and open the pot.
Close the Air Fryer Lid. Select BROIL, and set the time to 5 minutes. Select START to begin. Cook until top is browned.
Serve.

Air Fried Kale Chips

PREP: 5 MINUTES • COOK TIME: 10 MINUTES • TOTAL: 15 MINUTES
SERVES: 6

Ingredients
¼ tsp. Himalayan salt
3 tbsp. yeast
Avocado oil
1 bunch of kale

Directions:

1 **Preparing the Ingredients.** Rinse kale and with paper towels, dry well.
Tear kale leaves into large pieces. Remember they will shrink as they cook so good sized pieces are necessary.
Place kale pieces in a bowl and spritz with avocado oil till shiny. Sprinkle with salt and yeast.
With your hands, toss kale leaves well to combine.
2 **Air Frying.** Pour half of the kale mixture into the Foodi SmartLid, set temperature to 350°F, and set time to 5 minutes. Remove and repeat with another half of kale.

PER SERVING: CALORIES: 55; FAT: 10G; PROTEIN: 1G; SUGAR:0G

Zucchini Omelet

PREP: 10 MINUTES • COOK TIME: 10 MINUTES • TOTAL: 20 MINUTES
SERVES: 2

Ingredients
1 teaspoon butter
1 zucchini, julienned
4 eggs
¼ teaspoon fresh basil, chopped
¼ teaspoon red pepper flakes, crushed
Salt and freshly ground black pepper, to taste

Directions:

1 **Preparing the Ingredients.** Preheat the Foodi SmartLid to 355 degrees F.
In a skillet, melt butter on medium heat. Add zucchini and cook for about 3-4 minutes.
In a bowl, add the eggs, basil, red pepper flakes, salt and black pepper and beat well. Add cooked zucchini and gently, stir to combine.
2 **Air Frying.** Transfer the mixture into the Foodi SmartLid pan. Lock the air fryer lid. Cook for about 10 minutes or till done completely.

Cheesy Cauliflower Fritters

PREP: 10 MINUTES • COOK TIME: 7 MINUTES • TOTAL: 17 MINUTES
SERVES: 8

Ingredients
½ C. chopped parsley
1 C. Italian breadcrumbs
1/3 C. shredded mozzarella cheese
1/3 C. shredded sharp cheddar cheese
1 egg
2 minced garlic cloves
3 chopped scallions
1 head of cauliflower

Directions:
1. **Preparing the Ingredients.** Cut cauliflower up into florets. Wash well and pat dry. Place into a food processor and pulse 20-30 seconds till it looks like rice. Place cauliflower rice in a bowl and mix with pepper, salt, egg, cheeses, breadcrumbs, garlic, and scallions. With hands, form 15 patties of the mixture. Add more breadcrumbs if needed.
2. **Air Frying.** With olive oil, spritz patties, and place into your Foodi SmartLid in a single layer. Lock the air fryer lid. Set temperature to 390°F, and set time to 7 minutes, flipping after 7 minutes.

PER SERVING: CALORIES: 209; FAT: 17G; PROTEIN: 6G; SUGAR: 0.5

Cauliflower Bites

PREP: 10 MINUTES • COOK TIME: 18 MINUTES • TOTAL: 28 MINUTES
SERVES: 4

Ingredients
1 Head Cauliflower, cut into small florets
Tsps Garlic Powder
Pinch of Salt and Pepper
1 Tbsp Butter, melted
1/2 Cup Chili Sauce
Olive Oil

Directions:
1. **Preparing the Ingredients.** Place cauliflower into a bowl and pour oil over florets to lightly cover.
   Season florets with salt, pepper and the garlic powder and toss well.
2. **Air Frying.** Place florets into the Foodi SmartLid, lock the air fryer lid and set at 350 degrees for 14 minutes.
   Remove cauliflower from the Foodi SmartLid.
   Combine the melted butter with the chili sauce
   Pour over the florets so that they are well coated.
   Return to the Foodi SmartLid and cook for additional 3 to 4 minutes
   Serve as a side or with ranch or cheese dip as a snack

Buttered Carrot-Zucchini with Mayo

PREP: 10 MINUTES • **COOK TIME:** 25 MINUTES • **TOTAL:** 35 MINUTES
SERVES: 4

Ingredients
1 tablespoon grated onion
2 tablespoons butter, melted
1/2-pound carrots, sliced
1-1/2 zucchinis, sliced
1/4 cup water
1/4 cup mayonnaise
1/4 teaspoon prepared horseradish
1/4 teaspoon salt
1/4 teaspoon ground black pepper
1/4 cup Italian bread crumbs

Directions:
1. **Preparing the Ingredients.** Lightly grease baking pan of Foodi SmartLid with cooking spray. Add carrots. For 8 minutes, cook on 360°F. Add zucchini and continue cooking for another 5 minutes.
   Meanwhile, in a bowl whisk well pepper, salt, horseradish, onion, mayonnaise, and water. Pour into pan of veggies. Toss well to coat.
   In a small bowl mix melted butter and bread crumbs. Sprinkle over veggies.
2. **Air Frying.** Lock the air fryer lid. Cook for 10 minutes at 390°F, until tops are lightly browned.
   Serve and enjoy.

PER SERVING: CALORIES: 223; FAT: 17G; PROTEIN: 2.7G; SUGAR:0.5

Sage-Butter Spaghetti Squash

PREP: 5 MINUTES • **PRESSURE:** 12 MINUTES • **BROIL:** 22 MINUTES • **TOTAL:** 17 MINUTES • **PRESSURE LEVEL:** HIGH • **RELEASE:** QUICK
SERVES 6

Ingredients
One 3- to 3½-pound spaghetti squash, halved lengthwise and seeded
6 tablespoons unsalted butter
2 tablespoons packed fresh sage leaves, minced
½ teaspoon salt
½ teaspoon ground black pepper
½ cup finely grated Parmesan cheese (about 1 ounce)

Directions
1. **Preparing the Ingredients.** Put the squash cut side up in the cooker; add 1 cup water.
2. **High pressure for 12 minutes.** Lock the lid on the Foodi SmartLid and then cook for 12 minutes. To get 12-minutes cook time, press "Pressure" button, and use the Time Adjustment button to adjust the cook time to 12 minutes.
3. **Pressure Release.** Use the quick-release method to bring the pot's pressure back to normal.
4. **Finish the dish.** Unlock and open the cooker. Transfer the squash halves to a cutting board; cool for 10 minutes. Discard the liquid in the cooker. Use a fork to scrape the spaghetti-like flesh off the skin and onto the cutting board; discard the skins.
   Melt the butter in the electric cooker turned to its browning function. Stir in the sage, salt, and pepper, then add all of the squash. Stir and toss over the heat until

well combined and heated through about 2 minutes. Add the cheese, toss well.

5. Close the Air Fryer Lid. Select BROIL, and set the time to 5 minutes. Select START to begin. Cook until top is browned. Serve.

Roasted Vegetables Salad

PREP: 5 MINUTES • COOK TIME: 85 MINUTES • TOTAL: 90 MINUTES
SERVES: 5

Ingredients

3 eggplants
1 tbsp of olive oil
3 medium zucchini
1 tbsp of olive oil
4 large tomatoes, cut them in eighths
4 cups of one shaped pasta
2 peppers of any color
1 cup of sliced tomatoes cut into small cubes
2 teaspoon of salt substitute
8 tbsp of grated parmesan cheese
½ cup of Italian dressing
Leaves of fresh basil

Directions:

1. **Preparing the Ingredients.** Wash your eggplant and slice it off then discard the green end. Make sure not to peel.
Slice your eggplant into 1/2 inch of thick rounds. 1/2 inch)
Pour 1tbsp of olive oil on the eggplant round.

2. **Air Frying.** Put the eggplants in the basket of the Foodi SmartLid, lock the air fryer lid and then toss it in the Foodi SmartLid. Cook the eggplants for 40 minutes. Set the heat to 360 ° F
Meanwhile, wash your zucchini and slice it then discard the green end. But do not peel it.
Slice the Zucchini into thick rounds of ½ inch each.
In the basket of the Foodi SmartLid, toss your ingredients
Add 1 tbsp of olive oil.

3. **Air Frying.** Cook the zucchini for 25 minutes on a heat of 360° F and when the time is off set it aside.
Wash and cut the tomatoes.

4. **Air Frying.** Arrange your tomatoes in the basket of the Foodi SmartLid. Set the timer to 30 minutes. Set the heat to 350° F

   When the time is off, cook your pasta according to the pasta guiding directions, empty it into a colander. Run the cold water on it and wash it and drain the pasta and put it aside.

   Meanwhile, wash and chop your peppers and place it in a bow

   Wash and thinly slice your cherry tomatoes and add it to the bowl. Add your roasted veggies.

   Add the pasta, a pinch of salt, the topping dressing, add the basil and the parm and toss everything together. (It is better to mix with your hands). Set the ingredients together in the refrigerator, and let it chill

   Serve your salad and enjoy it!

Cheddar, Squash, And Zucchini Casserole

PREP: 5 MINUTES • COOK TIME: 30 MINUTES • TOTAL: 35 MINUTES
SERVES: 4

Ingredients

1 egg
5 saltine crackers, or as needed, crushed
2 tablespoons bread crumbs
1/2-pound yellow squash, sliced
1/2-pound zucchini, sliced
1/2 cup shredded Cheddar cheese
1-1/2 teaspoons white sugar
1/2 teaspoon salt
1/4 onion, diced
1/4 cup biscuit baking mix
1/4 cup butter

Directions:

1. **Preparing the Ingredients.** Lightly grease baking pan of Foodi SmartLid with cooking spray. Add onion, zucchini, and yellow squash. Cover pan with foil and for 15 minutes, cook on 360° F or until tender. Stir in salt, sugar, egg, butter, baking mix, and cheddar cheese. Mix well. Fold in crushed crackers. Top with bread crumbs.
2. **Air Frying** Lock the air fryer lid. Cook for 15 minutes at 390° F until tops are lightly browned.

   Serve and enjoy.

PER SERVING: CALORIES: 285; FAT: 20.5G; PROTEIN:8.6G

Zucchini Parmesan Chips

PREP: 10 MINUTES • COOK TIME: 8 MINUTES • TOTAL: 18 MINUTES
SERVES: 10

Ingredients
½ tsp. paprika
½ C. grated parmesan cheese
½ C. Italian breadcrumbs
1 lightly beaten egg
2 thinly sliced zucchinis

Directions:
1. **Preparing the Ingredients.** Use a very sharp knife or mandolin slicer to slice zucchini as thinly as you can. Pat off extra moisture.
Beat egg with a pinch of pepper and salt and a bit of water.
Combine paprika, cheese, and breadcrumbs in a bowl.
Dip slices of zucchini into the egg mixture and then into breadcrumb mixture. Press gently to coat.
2. **Air Frying.** With olive oil cooking spray, mist coated zucchini slices. Place into your Foodi SmartLid in a single layer. Lock the air fryer lid. Set temperature to 350°F, and set time to 8 minutes.
Sprinkle with salt and serve with salsa.

PER SERVING: CALORIES: 211; FAT: 16G; PROTEIN:8G; SUGAR:0G

Jalapeño Cheese Balls

PREP: 10 MINUTES • COOK TIME: 8 MINUTES • TOTAL: 18 MINUTES
SERVES: 12

Ingredients
4 ounces cream cheese
⅓ cup shredded mozzarella cheese
⅓ cup shredded Cheddar cheese
2 jalapeños, finely chopped
½ cup bread crumbs
2 eggs
½ cup all-purpose flour
Salt
Pepper
Cooking oil

Directions:
1. **Preparing the Ingredients.** In a medium bowl, combine the cream cheese, mozzarella, Cheddar, and jalapeños. Mix well.
Form the cheese mixture into balls about an inch thick. Using a small ice cream scoop works well.
Arrange the cheese balls on a sheet pan and place in the freezer for 15 minutes. This will help the cheese balls maintain their shape while frying.
Spray the Foodi SmartLid basket with cooking oil. Place the bread crumbs in a small bowl. In another small bowl, beat the eggs. In a third small bowl, combine the flour with salt and pepper to taste, and mix well. Remove the cheese balls from the freezer. Dip the cheese balls in the flour, then the eggs, and then the bread crumbs.
2. **Air Frying.** Place the cheese balls in the Foodi SmartLid. Spray with cooking oil. Lock the air fryer lid. Cook for 8 minutes.
Open the Foodi SmartLid and flip the cheese balls. I recommend flipping them instead of shaking so the balls maintain their form. Cook an additional 4 minutes. Cool before serving.

PER SERVING: CALORIES: 96; FAT: 6G; PROTEIN:4G; SUGAR:0G

Crispy Roasted Broccoli
PREP: 10 MINUTES • COOK TIME: 8 MINUTES • TOTAL: 18 MINUTES
SERVES: 2

Ingredients
¼ tsp. Masala
½ tsp. red chili powder
½ tsp. salt
¼ tsp. turmeric powder
1 tbsp. chickpea flour
2 tbsp. yogurt
1 pound broccoli

Directions:
1. **Preparing the Ingredients.** Cut broccoli up into florets. Soak in a bowl of water with 2 teaspoons of salt for at least half an hour to remove impurities.
   Take out broccoli florets from water and let drain. Wipe down thoroughly.
   Mix all other ingredients together to create a marinade.
   Toss broccoli florets in the marinade.
   Cover and chill 15-30 minutes.
2. **Air Frying.** Preheat the Foodi SmartLid to 390 degrees. Place marinated broccoli florets into the fryer, lock the air fryer lid, set temperature to 350°F, and set time to 10 minutes. Florets will be crispy when done.

PER SERVING: CALORIES: 96; FAT: 1.3G; PROTEIN:7G; SUGAR:4.5G

Creamy And Cheese Broccoli Bake

PREP: 5 MINUTES • COOK TIME: 30 MINUTES • TOTAL: 35 MINUTES
SERVES: 2

Ingredients
1-pound fresh broccoli, coarsely chopped
2 tablespoons all-purpose flour
salt to taste
1 tablespoon dry bread crumbs, or to taste
1/2 large onion, coarsely chopped
1/2 (14 ounce) can evaporated milk, divided
1/2 cup cubed sharp Cheddar cheese
1-1/2 teaspoons butter, or to taste
1/4 cup water

Directions:
1. **Preparing the Ingredients.** Lightly grease baking pan of Foodi SmartLid with cooking spray. Mix in half of the milk and flour in pan and for 5 minutes, cook on 360°F. Halfway through cooking time, mix well. Add broccoli and remaining milk. Mix well and cook for another 5 minutes.
Stir in cheese and mix well until melted.
In a small bowl mix well, butter and bread crumbs. Sprinkle on top of broccoli.
2. **Air Frying.** Lock the air fryer lid. Cook for 20 minutes at 360°F until tops are lightly browned.
Serve and enjoy.

PER SERVING: CALORIES: 444; FAT: 22.3G; PROTEIN:23G

Coconut Battered Cauliflower Bites

PREP: 5 MINUTES • COOK TIME: 20 MINUTES • TOTAL: 25 MINUTES
SERVES: 4

Ingredients
salt and pepper to taste
1 flax egg (1 tablespoon flaxseed meal + 3 tablespoon water)
1 small cauliflower, cut into florets
1 teaspoon mixed spice
½ teaspoon mustard powder
2 tablespoons maple syrup
1 clove of garlic, minced
2 tablespoons soy sauce
1/3 cup oats flour
1/3 cup plain flour
1/3 cup desiccated coconut

Directions:
1. **Preparing the Ingredients..**
In a mixing bowl, mix together oats, flour, and desiccated coconut. Season with salt and pepper to taste. Set aside.
In another bowl, place the flax egg and add a pinch of salt to taste. Set aside.
Season the cauliflower with mixed spice and mustard powder.
Dredge the florets in the flax egg first then in the flour mixture.
2. **Air Frying**. Place inside the Foodi SmartLid, lock the air fryer lid and cook at 400°F or 15 minutes.
Meanwhile, place the maple syrup, garlic, and soy sauce in a sauce pan and heat over medium flame. Bring to a boil and adjust the heat to low until the sauce thickens.
After 15 minutes, take out the florets from the Foodi SmartLid and place them in the saucepan.

Toss to coat the florets and place inside the Foodi SmartLid and cook for another 5 minutes.

PER SERVING: CALORIES: 154; FAT: 2.3G; PROTEIN:4.69G

Crispy Jalapeno Coins
PREP: 10 MINUTES • COOK TIME: 5 MINUTES • TOTAL: 15 MINUTES
SERVES: 2

Ingredients
1 egg
2-3 tbsp. coconut flour
1 sliced and seeded jalapeno
Pinch of garlic powder
Pinch of onion powder
Pinch of Cajun seasoning (optional)
Pinch of pepper and salt

Directions:
1. **Preparing the Ingredients.** Ensure your Foodi SmartLid is preheated to 400 degrees.
Mix together all dry ingredients.
Pat jalapeno slices dry. Dip coins into egg wash and then into dry mixture. Toss to thoroughly coat.
Add coated jalapeno slices to Foodi SmartLid in a singular layer. Spray with olive oil.
2. **Air Frying.** Lock the air fryer lid. Set temperature to 350°F, and set time to 5 minutes. Cook just till crispy.

PER SERVING: CALORIES: 128; FAT: 8G; PROTEIN:7G; SUGAR:0G

Buffalo Cauliflower

PREP: 5 MINUTES • COOK TIME: 15 MINUTES • TOTAL: 20 MINUTES
SERVES: 2

Ingredients
Cauliflower:
- 1 C. panko breadcrumbs
- 1 tsp. salt
- 4 C. cauliflower florets

Buffalo Coating:
- ¼ C. Vegan Buffalo sauce
- ¼ C. melted vegan butter

Directions:
1. **Preparing the Ingredients.** Melt butter in microwave and whisk in buffalo sauce. Dip each cauliflower floret into buffalo mixture, ensuring it gets coated well. Hold over a bowl till floret is done dripping. Mix breadcrumbs with salt.
2. **Air Frying.** Dredge dipped florets into breadcrumbs and place into Foodi SmartLid. Lock the air fryer lid. Set temperature to 350°F, and set time to 15 minutes. When slightly browned, they are ready to eat!
Serve with your favorite keto dipping sauce!

PER SERVING: CALORIES: 194; FAT: 17G; PROTEIN:10G; SUGAR:3

Crisped Baked Cheese Stuffed Chile Pepper

PREP: 10 MINUTES • COOK TIME: 30 MINUTES • TOTAL: 40 MINUTES
SERVES: 3

Ingredients
- 1 (7 ounce) can whole green Chile peppers, drained
- 1 egg, beaten
- 1 tablespoon all-purpose flour
- 1/2 (5 ounce) can evaporated milk
- 1/2 (8 ounce) can tomato sauce
- 1/4-pound Monterey Jack cheese, shredded
- 1/4-pound Longhorn or Cheddar cheese, shredded
- 1/4 cup milk

Directions:
1. **Preparing the Ingredients.** Lightly grease baking pan of Foodi SmartLid with cooking spray. Evenly spread chilies and sprinkle cheddar and Jack cheese on top.
In a bowl whisk well flour, milk, and eggs. Pour over chilies.
2. **Air Frying.** Lock the air fryer lid. For 20 minutes, cook on 360°F
Add tomato sauce on top.
Cook for 10 minutes at 390°F until tops are lightly browned.
Serve and enjoy.

PER SERVING: CALORIES: 392; FAT: 27.6G; PROTEIN:23.9G

Jicama Fries

PREP: 10 MINUTES • COOK TIME: 5 MINUTES • TOTAL: 15 MINUTES
SERVES: 8

Ingredients
1 tbsp. dried thyme
¾ C. arrowroot flour
½ large Jicama
eggs

Directions:
1. **Preparing the Ingredients.** Sliced jicama into fries.
   Whisk eggs together and pour over fries. Toss to coat.
   Mix a pinch of salt, thyme, and arrowroot flour together. Toss egg-coated jicama into dry mixture, tossing to coat well.
2. **Air Frying.** Spray the Foodi SmartLid basket with olive oil and add fries. Lock the air fryer lid. Set temperature to 350°F, and set time to 5 minutes. Toss halfway into the cooking process.

PER SERVING: CALORIES: 211; FAT: 19G; PROTEIN:9G; SUGAR:1

Jumbo Stuffed Mushrooms

PREP: 10 MINUTES • COOK TIME: 20 MINUTES • TOTAL: 30 MINUTES
SERVES: 4

Ingredients
4 jumbo portobello mushrooms
1 tablespoon olive oil
¼ cup ricotta cheese
5 tablespoons Parmesan cheese, divided
1 cup frozen chopped spinach, thawed and drained
⅓ cup bread crumbs
¼ teaspoon minced fresh rosemary

Directions:
1. **Preparing the Ingredients.** Wipe the mushrooms with a damp cloth. Remove the stems and discard. Using a spoon, gently scrape out most of the gills.
   Rub the mushrooms with the olive oil.
2. **Air Frying** Put in the Foodi SmartLid basket, hollow side up, lock the air fryer lid and bake for 3 minutes. Carefully remove the mushroom caps, because they will contain liquid. Drain the liquid out of the caps.
   In a medium bowl, combine the ricotta, 3 tablespoons of Parmesan cheese, spinach, bread crumbs, and rosemary, and mix well. Stuff this mixture into the drained mushroom caps. Sprinkle with the remaining 2 tablespoons of Parmesan cheese.
   Put the mushroom caps back into the basket and bake for 4 to 6 minutes or until the filling is hot and the mushroom caps are tender.

PER SERVING: CALORIES: 117; FAT: 7G; PROTEIN:7G; FIBER:1G

Air Fryer Brussels Sprouts

PREP: 10 MINUTES • COOK TIME: 10 MINUTES • TOTAL: 20 MINUTES
SERVES: 8

Ingredients
¼ tsp. salt
1 tbsp. balsamic vinegar
1 tbsp. olive oil
2 C. Brussels sprouts

Directions:
1. **Preparing the Ingredients.** Cut Brussels sprouts in half lengthwise. Toss with salt, vinegar, and olive oil till coated thoroughly.
2. **Air Frying.** Add coated sprouts to the Foodi SmartLid, close air fryer lid, set temperature to 400°F, and set time to 10 minutes. Shake after 5 minutes of cooking. Brussels sprouts are ready to devour when brown and crisp!

PER SERVING: CALORIES: 118; FAT: 9G; PROTEIN:11G; SUGAR:1

Spaghetti Squash Tots

PREP: 10 MINUTES • COOK TIME: 15 MINUTES • TOTAL: 25 MINUTES
SERVES: 8

Ingredients
¼ tsp. pepper
½ tsp. salt
1 thinly sliced scallion
1 spaghetti squash

Directions:
1. **Preparing the Ingredients.** Wash and cut the squash in half lengthwise. Scrape out the seeds.
   With a fork, remove spaghetti meat by strands and throw out skins.
   In a clean towel, toss in squash and wring out as much moisture as possible. Place in a bowl and with a knife slice through meat a few times to cut up smaller.
   Add pepper, salt, and scallions to squash and mix well.
2. **Air Frying.** Create "tot" shapes with your hands and place in the Foodi SmartLid. Spray with olive oil. Lock the air fryer lid. Set temperature to 350°F, and set time to 15 minutes. Cook until golden and crispy!

PER SERVING: CALORIES: 231; FAT: 18G; PROTEIN:5G; SUGAR:0G

Crispy And Healthy Avocado Fingers

PREP: 10 MINUTES • COOK TIME: 10 MINUTES • TOTAL: 20 MINUTES
SERVES: 4

Ingredients
½ cup panko breadcrumbs
½ teaspoon salt
1 pitted Haas avocado, peeled and sliced
liquid from 1 can white beans or aquafaba

Directions:
1. **Preparing the Ingredients.** Preheat the Foodi SmartLid at 350°F.
   In a shallow bowl, toss the breadcrumbs and salt until well combined.
   Dredge the avocado slices first with the aquafaba then in the breadcrumb mixture. Place the avocado slices in a single layer inside the Foodi SmartLid basket.
2. **Air Frying.** Lock the air fryer lid. Cook for 10 minutes and shake halfway through the cooking time.

PER SERVING: CALORIES: 51; FAT: 7.5G; PROTEIN:1.39G

Onion Rings

PREP: 10 MINUTES • COOK TIME: 10 MINUTES • TOTAL: 20 MINUTES
SERVES: 4

Ingredients
1 large spanish onion
1/2 cup buttermilk
2 eggs, lightly beaten
3/4 cups unbleached all-purpose flour
3/4 cups panko bread crumbs
1/2 teaspoon baking powder
1/2 teaspoon Cayenne pepper, to taste
Salt

Directions:
1. **Preparing the Ingredients.** Start by cutting your onion into 1/2 thick rings and separate. Smaller pieces can be discarded or saved for other recipes.
   Beat the eggs in a large bowl and mix in the buttermilk, then set it aside.
   In another bowl combine flour, pepper, bread crumbs, and baking powder.
   Use a large spoon to dip a whole ring in the buttermilk, then pull it through the flour mix on both sides to completely coat the ring.
2. **Air Frying.** Lock the air fryer lid. Cook about 8 rings at a time in your Foodi SmartLid for 8-10 minutes at 360 degrees shaking half way through.

PER SERVING: CALORIES: 225; FAT: 3.8G; PROTEIN:19G; FIBER:2.4G

Cinnamon Butternut Squash Fries

PREP: 5 MINUTES • COOK TIME: 10 MINUTES • TOTAL: 15 MINUTES
SERVES: 8

Ingredients
1 pinch of salt
1 tbsp. powdered unprocessed sugar
½ tsp. nutmeg
2 tsp. cinnamon
1 tbsp. coconut oil
10 ounces pre-cut butternut squash fries

Directions:
1. **Preparing the Ingredients.** In a plastic bag, pour in all ingredients. Coat fries with other components till coated and sugar is dissolved.
2. **Air Frying.** Spread coated fries into a single layer in the Foodi SmartLid. Lock the air fryer lid. Set temperature to 390°F, and set time to 10 minutes. Cook until crispy.

PER SERVING: CALORIES: 175; FAT: 8G; PROTEIN:1G; SUGAR

Poultry Recipes

Korean Chicken Wings

PREP: 5 MINUTES • COOK TIME: 10 MINUTES • TOTAL: 15 MINUTES
SERVES: 8

Ingredients
Wings:
1 tsp. pepper
1 tsp. salt
2 pounds chicken wings
Sauce:
2 packets Splenda
1 tbsp. minced garlic
1 tbsp. minced ginger
1 tbsp. sesame oil
1 tsp. agave nectar
1 tbsp. mayo
2 tbsp. gochujang
Finishing:
¼ C. chopped green onions
2 tsp. sesame seeds

Directions:
1. **Preparing the Ingredients.** Ensure Foodi SmartLid is preheated to 400 degrees. Line a small pan with foil and place a rack onto the pan, then place into Foodi SmartLid.
Season wings with pepper and salt and place onto the rack.
2. **Air Frying.** Lock the air fryer lid. Set temperature to 160°F, and set time to 20 minutes and air fry 20 minutes, turning at 10 minutes.
As chicken air fries, mix together all the sauce components.
Once a thermometer says that the chicken has reached 160 degrees, take out wings and place into a bowl.
Pour half of the sauce mixture over wings, tossing well to coat.
Put coated wings back into Foodi SmartLid for 5 minutes or till they reach 165 degrees.
Remove and sprinkle with green onions and sesame seeds. Dip into extra sauce.

PER SERVING: CALORIES: 356; FAT: 26G; PROTEIN:23G; SUGAR:2G

Enchilada-Braised Chicken Breasts

PREP: 5 MINUTES • PRESSURE: 15 MINUTES • AIR CRISP: 9 MINUTES • TOTAL: 29 MINUTES • PRESSURE LEVEL: HIGH • RELEASE: QUICK
SERVES 4

Ingredients
1 teaspoon packed dark brown sugar
1 teaspoon ground cumin
1 teaspoon smoked paprika
½ teaspoon salt
½ teaspoon ground black pepper
½ teaspoon onion powder
¼ teaspoon garlic powder
Four 6- to 8-ounce boneless skinless chicken breasts
2 tablespoons olive oil
One 8-ounce can tomato sauce (1 cup)
½ cup light-colored beer, preferably a Pilsner or an IPA
2 tablespoons chili powder
2 tablespoons fresh lime juice

Directions
1. **Preparing the Ingredients.** Mix the brown sugar, cumin, smoked paprika, salt, pepper, onion powder, and garlic powder in a medium bowl. Massage the spice rub onto the chicken breasts.
   Heat the oil in the Foodi SmartLid using the "Sauté" function. Set the breasts in the cooker and brown well, turning once, about 6 minutes.
   Mix the tomato sauce, beer, chili powder, and lime juice in the bowl the spices were in; pour the sauce over the breasts.
2. **High pressure for 15 minutes.** Close the pressure cooking lid and Cook for 15 minutes. To get 15-minutes cook time, press the "Pressure" Button and adjust the time.
3. **Pressure Release.** Use the quick-release method to bring the pot's pressure back to normal.
   Close the Air Fryer Lid. Select AIR FRY, set temperature to 390°F, and set time to 9 minutes. Check after 6 minutes, cooking for an additional 3 minutes if dish needs more browning. Serve the chicken with the sauce ladled on top.

Sweet And Sour Chicken

PREP: 5 MINUTES • COOK TIME: 20 MINUTES • TOTAL: 25 MINUTES
SERVES: 6

Ingredients
3 Chicken Breasts, cubed
1/2 Cup Flour
1/2 Cup Cornstarch
2 Red Peppers, sliced
1 Onion, chopped
2 Carrots, julienned
3/4 Cup Sugar
2 Tbsps Cornstarch
1/3 Cup Vinegar
2/3 Cup Water
1/4 cup Soy sauce
1 Tbsp Ketchup

Directions:
1. **Preparing the Ingredients.** Preheat the Foodi SmartLid to 375 degrees.
Combine the flour, cornstarch and chicken in an air tight container and shake to combine
Remove chicken from the container and shake off any excess flour.
2. **Air Frying.** Add chicken to the Foodi SmartLid tray and cook for 20 minutes.
In a saucepan, whisk together sugar, water, vinegar, soy sauce and ketchup.
Bring to a boil over medium heat, reduce the heat then simmer for 2 minutes
After cooking the chicken for 20 minutes, add the vegetables and sauce mixture to the Foodi SmartLid and cook for another 5 minutes
Serve over hot rice

Perfect Chicken Parmesan

PREP: 5 MINUTES • COOK TIME: 25 MINUTES • TOTAL: 30 MINUTES
SERVES: 2

Ingredients
2 large white meat chicken breasts, approximately 5-6 ounces
1 cup of breadcrumbs (Panko brand works well)
2 medium-sized eggs
Pinch of salt and pepper
1 tablespoon of dried oregano
1 cup of marinara sauce (store-bought or homemade will do equally well)
2 slices of provolone cheese
1 tablespoon of parmesan cheese

Directions:
1. **Preparing the Ingredients.** Cover the basket of the Foodi SmartLid with a lining of tin foil, leaving the edges uncovered to allow air to circulate through the basket. Preheat the Foodi SmartLid to 350 degrees.
In a mixing bowl, beat the eggs until fluffy and until the yolks and whites are fully combined, and set aside.
In a separate mixing bowl, combine the breadcrumbs, oregano, salt and pepper, and set aside.
One by one, dip the raw chicken breasts into the bowl with dry ingredients, coating both sides; then submerge into the bowl with wet ingredients, then dip again into the dry ingredients. This double coating will ensure an extra crisp-and-delicious air-fry!
Lay the coated chicken breasts on the foil covering the Foodi SmartLid basket, in a single flat layer.
2. **Air Frying.** Lock the air fryer lid. Set the Foodi SmartLid timer for 10 minutes.

After 10 minutes, the Foodi SmartLid will turn off and the chicken should be midway cooked and the breaded coating starting to brown.

Using tongs, turn each piece of chicken over to ensure a full all-over fry.

Reset the Foodi SmartLid to 320 degrees for another 10 minutes.

While the chicken is cooking, pour half the marinara sauce into a 7-inch heat-safe pan.

After 15 minutes, when the Foodi SmartLid shuts off, remove the fried chicken breasts using tongs and set in the marinara-covered pan. Drizzle the rest of the marinara sauce over the fried chicken, then place the slices of provolone cheese atop both of them and sprinkle the parmesan cheese over the entire pan.

Reset the Foodi SmartLid to 350 degrees for 5 minutes.

After 5 minutes, when the Foodi SmartLid shuts off, remove the dish from the Foodi SmartLid using tongs or oven mitts. The chicken will be perfectly crisped and the cheese melted and lightly toasted. Serve while hot!

Basil-Garlic Breaded Chicken Bake

PREP: 5 MINUTES • COOK TIME: 25 MINUTES • TOTAL: 30 MINUTES
SERVES: 2

Ingredients
2 boneless skinless chicken breast halves (4 ounces each)
1 tablespoon butter, melted
1 large tomato, seeded and chopped
2 garlic cloves, minced
1 1/2 tablespoons minced fresh basil
1/2 tablespoon olive oil
1/2 teaspoon salt
1/4 cup all-purpose flour
1/4 cup egg substitute
1/4 cup grated Parmesan cheese
1/4 cup dry bread crumbs
1/4 teaspoon pepper

Directions:

1. **Preparing the Ingredients.** In shallow bowl, whisk well egg substitute and place flour in a separate bowl. Dip chicken in flour, then egg, and then flour. In small bowl whisk well butter, bread crumbs and cheese. Sprinkle over chicken.

   Lightly grease baking pan of Foodi SmartLid with cooking spray. Place breaded chicken on bottom of pan. Cover with foil.

2. **Air Frying.** Lock the air fryer lid. For 20 minutes, cook on 390°F.

   Meanwhile, in a bowl whisk well remaining ingredient.

   Remove foil from pan and then pour over chicken the remaining Ingredients.

   Cook for 8 minutes.

   Serve and enjoy.

PER SERVING: CALORIES: 311; FAT: 11G; PROTEIN:31G; CARBS:22G

Honey-Chipotle Chicken Wings

PREP: 5 MINUTES • PRESSURE: 10 MINUTES • AIR CRISP: 10 MINUTES • TOTAL: 25 MINUTES • PRESSURE LEVEL: HIGH • RELEASE: QUICK
SERVES 2

Ingredients

1 cup water, for steaming
3 tablespoons Mexican hot sauce (such as Valentina brand)
2 tablespoons honey
1 teaspoon minced canned chipotle in adobo sauce

Directions

1. **Preparing the Ingredients**. If using whole wings, cut off the tips and discard. Cut the wings at the joint into two pieces each, the "drumette" and the "flat."
Add the water and insert the steamer basket or trivet. Place the wings on the steamer insert.
2. **High pressure for 10 minutes**. Close the pressure cooking lid and the pressure valve and then cook for 10 minutes. To get 10-minutes cook time, press "Pressure" button and the time selector.
3. **Pressure Release**. Use the quick-release method.
4. **Finish the dish**. While the wings are cooking, make the sauce. In a large bowl, whisk together the hot sauce, honey, and minced chipotle.
5. Close the Air Fryer lid. Select AIR FRY, set temperature to 390°F, and set time to 10 minutes. Select START to begin.

PER SERVING: CALORIES: 434; FAT: 27G; SODIUM: 1,152MG; CARBOHYDRATES: 19G; FIBER: 1G; PROTEIN: 31G

Buffalo Chicken Wings

PREP: 5 MINUTES • COOK TIME: 30 MINUTES • TOTAL: 35 MINUTES
SERVES: 8

Ingredients

1 tsp. salt
1-2 tbsp. brown sugar
1 tbsp. Worcestershire sauce
½ C. vegan butter
½ C. cayenne pepper sauce
4 pounds chicken wings

Directions:

1. **Preparing the Ingredients**. Whisk salt, brown sugar, Worcestershire sauce, butter, and hot sauce together and set to the side.
Dry wings and add to Foodi SmartLid basket.
2. **Air Frying.** Lock the air fryer lid. Set temperature to 380°F, and set time to 25 minutes. Cook tossing halfway through. When timer sounds, shake wings and bump up the temperature to 400 degrees and cook another 5 minutes.
Take out wings and place into a big bowl. Add sauce and toss well.
Serve alongside celery sticks!

PER SERVING: CALORIES: 402; FAT: 16G; PROTEIN:17G; SUGAR:4G

Honey and Wine Chicken Breasts

PREP: 5 MINUTES • COOK TIME: 15 MINUTES • TOTAL: 20 MINUTES
SERVES: 4

Ingredients

2 chicken breasts, rinsed and halved
1 tablespoon melted butter
1/2 teaspoon freshly ground pepper, or to taste
3/4 teaspoon sea salt, or to taste
1 teaspoon paprika
1 teaspoon dried rosemary
2 tablespoons dry white wine
1 tablespoon honey

Directions:
1. **Preparing the Ingredients.** Firstly, pat the chicken breasts dry. Lightly coat them with the melted butter.
   Then, add the remaining ingredients.
2. **Air Frying.** Transfer them to the Foodi SmartLid basket; Lock the air fryer lid, bake about 15 minutes at 330 degrees F. Serve warm and enjoy!
3.

PER SERVING: CALORIES: 189; FAT: 14G; PROTEIN:11G; SUGAR:1G

Chicken Fajitas

PREP: 10 MINUTES • COOK TIME: 10 MINUTES • TOTAL: 20 MINUTES
SERVES: 4

Ingredients

4 boneless, skinless chicken breasts, sliced
1 small red onion, sliced
2 red bell peppers, sliced
½ cup spicy ranch salad dressing, divided
½ teaspoon dried oregano
8 corn tortillas
2 cups torn butter lettuce
2 avocados, peeled and chopped

Directions:

1. **Preparing the Ingredients.** Place the chicken, onion, and pepper in the Foodi SmartLid basket. Drizzle with 1 tablespoon of the salad dressing and add the oregano. Toss to combine.

2. **Air Frying.** Grill for 10 to 14 minutes or until the chicken is 165°F on a food thermometer. Transfer the chicken and vegetables to a bowl and toss with the remaining salad dressing. Serve the chicken mixture with the tortillas, lettuce, and avocados and let everyone make their own creations.

PER SERVING: CALORIES: 783; FAT: 38G; PROTEIN:72; FIBER:12G

Crispy Honey Garlic Chicken Wings

PREP: 10 MINUTES • COOK TIME: 25 MINUTES • TOTAL: 35 MINUTES
SERVES: 8

Ingredients
1/8 C. water
½ tsp. salt
4 tbsp. minced garlic
¼ C. vegan butter
¼ C. raw honey
¾ C. almond flour
16 chicken wings

Directions:
1. **Preparing the Ingredients.** Rinse off and dry chicken wings well.
Spray Foodi SmartLid basket with olive oil.
Coat chicken wings with almond flour and add coated wings to Foodi SmartLid.
2. **Air Frying.** Set temperature to 380°F, and set time to 25 minutes. Cook shaking every 5 minutes.
When the timer goes off, cook 5-10 minutes at 400 degrees till skin becomes crispy and dry.
As chicken cooks, melt butter in a saucepan and add garlic. Sauté garlic 5 minutes. Add salt and honey, simmering 20 minutes. Make sure to stir every so often, so the sauce does not burn. Add a bit of water after 15 minutes to ensure sauce does not harden.
Take out chicken wings from Foodi SmartLid and coat in sauce. Enjoy!

PER SERVING: CALORIES: 435; FAT: 19G; PROTEIN:31G; SUGAR:6G

Zingy & Nutty Chicken Wings

PREP: 5 MINUTES • COOK TIME: 18 MINUTES • TOTAL: 23 MINUTES
SERVES: 4

Ingredients
1 tablespoon fish sauce
1 tablespoon fresh lemon juice
1 teaspoon sugar
12 chicken middle wings, cut into half
2 fresh lemongrass stalks, chopped finely
¼ cup unsalted cashews, crushed

Directions:
1. **Preparing the Ingredients.** In a bowl, mix together fish sauce, lime juice and sugar.
Add wings ad coat with mixture generously. Refrigerate to marinate for about 1-2 hours.
Preheat the Foodi SmartLid to 355 degrees F.
2. **Air Frying.** In the Foodi SmartLid pan, place lemongrass stalks. Lock the air fryer lid. Cook for about 2-3 minutes. Remove the cashew mixture from Foodi SmartLid and transfer into a bowl. Now, set the Foodi SmartLid to 390 degrees F.
Place the chicken wings in Foodi SmartLid pan. Cook for about 13-15 minutes further.
Transfer the wings into serving plates. Sprinkle with cashew mixture and serve.

Chicken Fillets, Brie & Ham

PREP: 5 MINUTES • COOK TIME: 15 MINUTES • TOTAL: 20 MINUTES
SERVES: 4

Ingredients

2 Large Chicken Fillets
Freshly Ground Black Pepper
4 Small Slices of Brie (Or your cheese of choice)
1 Tbsp Freshly Chopped Chives
4 Slices Cured Ham

Directions:
1. **Preparing the Ingredients**. Slice the fillets into four and make incisions as you would for a hamburger bun. Leave a little "hinge" uncut at the back. Season the inside and pop some brie and chives in there. Close them, and wrap them each in a slice of ham. Brush with oil and pop them into the basket.
2. **Air Frying**. Heat the Foodi SmartLid to 350° F. Lock the air fryer lid. Roast the little parcels until they look tasty (15 min)

Ricotta and Parsley Stuffed Turkey Breasts
PREP: 5 MINUTES • COOK TIME: 25 MINUTES • TOTAL: 30 MINUTES
SERVES: 4

Ingredients
1 turkey breast, quartered
1 cup Ricotta cheese
1/4 cup fresh Italian parsley, chopped
1 teaspoon garlic powder
1/2 teaspoon cumin powder
1 egg, beaten
1 teaspoon paprika
Salt and ground black pepper, to taste
Crushed tortilla chips
1 ½ tablespoons extra-virgin olive oil

Directions:
1. **Preparing the Ingredients.** Firstly, flatten out each piece of turkey breast with a rolling pin. Prepare three mixing bowls.
   In a shallow bowl, combine Ricotta cheese with the parsley, garlic powder, and cumin powder.
   Place the Ricotta/parsley mixture in the middle of each piece. Repeat with the remaining pieces of the turkey breast and roll them up.
   In another shallow bowl, whisk the egg together with paprika. In the third shallow bowl, combine the salt, pepper, and crushed tortilla chips.
   Dip each roll in the whisked egg, then, roll them over the tortilla chips mixture. Transfer prepared rolls to the basket. Drizzle olive oil over all.
2. **Air Frying.** Lock the air fryer lid. Cook at 350 degrees F for 25 minutes, working in batches. Serve warm, garnished with some extra parsley, if desired.

Chicken-Fried Steak Supreme
PREP: 10 MINUTES • COOK TIME: 30 MINUTES • TOTAL: 40 MINUTES
SERVES: 8

Ingredients
½ pound beef-bottom round, sliced into strips
1 cup of breadcrumbs (Panko brand works well)
2 medium-sized eggs

Pinch of salt and pepper
½ tablespoon of ground thyme

Directions:

1. **Preparing the Ingredients.** Cover the basket of the Foodi SmartLid with a lining of tin foil, leaving the edges uncovered to allow air to circulate through the basket. Preheat the Foodi SmartLid to 350 degrees. In a mixing bowl, beat the eggs until fluffy and until the yolks and whites are fully combined, and set aside. In a separate mixing bowl, combine the breadcrumbs, thyme, salt and pepper, and set aside. One by one, dip each piece of raw steak into the bowl with dry ingredients, coating all sides; then submerge into the bowl with wet ingredients, then dip again into the dry ingredients. This double coating will ensure an extra crisp air fry. Lay the coated steak pieces on the foil covering the air-fryer basket, in a single flat layer.
2. **Air Frying.** Set the Foodi SmartLid timer for 15 minutes. Lock the air fryer lid. After 15 minutes, the Foodi SmartLid will turn off and the steak should be mid-way cooked and the breaded coating starting to brown. Using tongs, turn each piece of steak over to ensure a full all-over fry. Reset the Foodi SmartLid to 320 degrees for 15 minutes. After 15 minutes, when the Foodi SmartLid shuts off, remove the fried steak strips using tongs and set on a serving plate. Eat as soon as cool enough to handle and enjoy!

Cheesy Chicken Tenders
PREP: 10 MINUTES • COOK TIME: 30 MINUTES • TOTAL: 40 MINUTES
SERVES: 4

Ingredients
1 large white meat chicken breast, approximately 5-6 ounces, sliced into strips
1 cup of breadcrumbs (Panko brand works well)
2 medium-sized eggs
Pinch of salt and pepper
1 tablespoon of grated or powdered parmesan cheese

Directions:

1. **Preparing the Ingredients.** Cover the basket of the Foodi SmartLid with a lining of tin foil, leaving the edges uncovered to allow air to circulate through the basket. Preheat the Foodi SmartLid to 350 degrees. In a mixing bowl, beat the eggs until fluffy and until the yolks and whites are fully combined, and set aside. In a separate mixing bowl, combine the breadcrumbs, parmesan, salt and pepper, and set aside. One by one, dip each piece of raw chicken into the bowl with dry ingredients, coating all sides; then submerge into the bowl with wet ingredients, then dip again into the dry ingredients. Lay the coated chicken pieces on the foil covering the Foodi SmartLid basket, in a single flat layer.
2. **Air Frying.** Set the Foodi SmartLid timer for 15 minutes. After 15 minutes, the Foodi SmartLid will turn off and the chicken should be mid-way cooked and the breaded coating starting to brown. Using tongs turn each piece of chicken over to ensure a full all over fry. Reset the

Foodi SmartLid to 320 degrees for another 15 minutes. After 15 minutes, when the Foodi SmartLid shuts off, remove the fried chicken strips using tongs and set on a serving plate. Eat as soon as cool enough to handle, and enjoy!

PER SERVING: CALORIES: 278; FAT: 15G; PROTEIN:29G; SUGAR:7G

Lemon-Pepper Chicken Wings

PREP: 10 MINUTES • COOK TIME: 20 MINUTES • TOTAL: 30 MINUTES

SERVES: 4

Ingredients

8 whole chicken wings
Juice of ½ lemon
½ teaspoon garlic powder
1 teaspoon onion powder
Salt
Pepper
¼ cup low-fat buttermilk
½ cup all-purpose flour
Cooking oil

Directions:

1. **Preparing the Ingredients.** Place the wings in a sealable plastic bag. Drizzle the wings with the lemon juice. Season the wings with the garlic powder, onion powder, and salt and pepper to taste.
Seal the bag. Shake thoroughly to combine the seasonings and coat the wings.
Pour the buttermilk and the flour into separate bowls large enough to dip the wings.
Spray the Foodi SmartLid basket with cooking oil.
One at a time, dip the wings in the buttermilk and then the flour.
2. **Air Frying.** Place the wings in the Foodi SmartLid basket. It is okay to stack them on top of each other. Spray the wings with cooking oil, being sure to spray the bottom layer. Lock the air fryer lid. Cook for 5 minutes.
Remove the basket and shake it to ensure all of the pieces will cook fully.
Return the basket to the Foodi SmartLid and continue to cook the chicken. Repeat shaking every 5 minutes until a total of 20 minutes has passed.
Cool before serving.

PER SERVING: CALORIES: 347; FAT: 12G; PROTEIN:46G; FIBER:1G

Easy Turkey Breast

PREP: 10 MINUTES • PRESSURE: 60 MINUTES • TOTAL: 70 MINUTES • PRESSURE LEVEL: HIGH • RELEASE: NATURAL
SERVES 4

Ingredients
1 frozen turkey breast with frozen gravy packet
1 whole onion

Directions
1. **Preparing the Ingredients.** Place frozen turkey breast, frozen gravy packet and whole onion in the Foodi SmartLid.
2. **High pressure for 30 minutes.** Lock the pressure cooking lid on the Foodi SmartLid and then cook for 30 minutes. To get 30-minutes cook time, press "Pressure" button and use the Time Adjustment button to adjust the cook time to 30 minutes.
3. **Pressure Release.** Use natural-release method.
   Remove lid, turn turkey breast over
4. **High pressure for 30 minutes.** Replace pressure cooking lid on the Foodi SmartLid and then cook for 30 minutes. To get 30-minutes cook time, press "Pressure" button
   and use the Time Adjustment button to adjust the cook time to 30 minutes.
5. **Pressure Release.** Use natural-release method, again.
6. **Finish the dish.** Close Air fryer lid. Select AIR FRY, set temperature to 360°F, and set time to 10 minutes. Check after 5 minutes, cooking for an additional 5 minutes if dish needs more browning.
   Remove mesh. Remove turkey and slice. Places slices and turkey gravy into serving dish.

Caesar Marinated Grilled Chicken

PREP: 10 MINUTES • COOK TIME: 24 MINUTES • TOTAL: 34 MINUTES
SERVES: 3

Ingredients
¼ cup crouton
1 teaspoon lemon zest. Form into ovals, skewer and grill.
1/2 cup Parmesan
1/4 cup breadcrumbs
1-pound ground chicken
2 tablespoons Caesar dressing and more for drizzling
2-4 romaine leaves

Directions:
1. **Preparing the Ingredients.** In a shallow dish, mix well chicken, 2 tablespoons Caesar dressing, parmesan, and breadcrumbs. Mix well with hands. Form into 1-inch oval patties.
   Thread chicken pieces in skewers. Place on skewer rack in Foodi SmartLid.
2. **Air Frying.** Lock the air fryer lid. For 12 minutes, cook on 360°F. Halfway through cooking time, turnover skewers. If needed, cook in batches.
   Serve and enjoy on a bed of lettuce and sprinkle with croutons and extra dressing.

PER SERVING: CALORIES: 339; FAT: 18.9G; PROTEIN:32.6G; SUGAR:1G

Minty Chicken-Fried Pork Chops

PREP: 10 MINUTES • COOK TIME: 30 MINUTES • TOTAL: 40 MINUTES
SERVES: 6

Ingredients

4 medium-sized pork chops, approximately 3.5 ounces each
1 cup of breadcrumbs (Panko brand works well)
2 medium-sized eggs
Pinch of salt and pepper
½ tablespoon of mint, either dried and ground; or fresh, rinsed, and finely chopped

Directions:

1. **Preparing the Ingredients.** Cover the basket of the Foodi SmartLid with a lining of tin foil, leaving the edges uncovered to allow air to circulate through the basket. Preheat the Foodi SmartLid to 350 degrees.
   In a mixing bowl, beat the eggs until fluffy and until the yolks and whites are fully combined, and set aside.
   In a separate mixing bowl, combine the breadcrumbs, mint, salt and pepper, and set aside. One by one, dip each raw pork chop into the bowl with dry ingredients, coating all sides; then submerge into the bowl with wet ingredients, then dip again into the dry ingredients. This double coating will ensure an extra crisp air-fry. Lay the coated pork chops on the foil covering the Foodi SmartLid basket, in a single flat layer.
2. **Air Frying.** Lock the air fryer lid. Set the Foodi SmartLid timer for 15 minutes. After 15 minutes, the Foodi SmartLid will turn off and the pork should be mid-way cooked and the breaded coating starting to brown. Using tongs, turn each piece of steak over to ensure a full all-over fry. Reset the Foodi SmartLid to 320 degrees for 15 minutes.

After 15 minutes, when the Foodi SmartLid shuts off, remove the fried pork chops using tongs and set on a serving plate. Eat as soon as cool enough to handle – and enjoy!

Crispy Southern Fried Chicken

PREP: 10 MINUTES • COOK TIME: 25 MINUTES • TOTAL: 35 MINUTES
SERVES: 4

Ingredients
1 tsp. cayenne pepper
2 tbsp. mustard powder
2 tbsp. oregano
2 tbsp. thyme
3 tbsp. coconut milk
1 beaten egg
¼ C. cauliflower
¼ C. gluten-free oats
8 chicken drumsticks

Directions:
1 **Preparing the Ingredients.** Ensure the Foodi SmartLid is preheated to 350 degrees.
   Lay out chicken and season with pepper and salt on all sides.
   Add all other ingredients to a blender, blending till a smooth-like breadcrumb mixture is created. Place in a bowl and add a beaten egg to another bowl.
   Dip chicken into breadcrumbs, then into egg, and breadcrumbs once more.
2 **Air Frying.** Place coated drumsticks into the Foodi SmartLid. Lock the air fryer lid. Set temperature to 350°F, and set time to 20 minutes and cook 20 minutes. Bump up the temperature to 390 degrees and cook another 5 minutes till crispy.

PER SERVING: CALORIES: 504; FAT: 18G; PROTEIN:35G; SUGAR:5G

Chicken Roast with Pineapple Salsa

PREP: 10 MINUTES • COOK TIME: 45 MINUTES • TOTAL: 55 MINUTES
SERVES: 2

Ingredients
¼ cup extra virgin olive oil
¼ cup freshly chopped cilantro
1 avocado, diced
1-pound boneless chicken breasts
2 cups canned pineapples
2 teaspoons honey
Juice from 1 lime
Salt and pepper to taste

Directions:
1 **Preparing the Ingredients.** Preheat the Foodi SmartLid to 390°F.
   Place the grill pan accessory in the Foodi SmartLid.
   Season the chicken breasts with lime juice, olive oil, honey, salt, and pepper.
2 **Air Frying.** Place on the grill pan, lock the air fryer lid and cook for 45 minutes.
   Flip the chicken every 10 minutes to grill all sides evenly.
   Once the chicken is cooked, serve with pineapples, cilantro, and avocado.

PER SERVING: CALORIES: 744; FAT: 32.8G; PROTEIN:4.7G; SUGAR:5G

Tex-Mex Turkey Burgers

PREP: 10 MINUTES • COOK TIME: 15 MINUTES • TOTAL: 25 MINUTES
SERVES: 4

Ingredients
⅓ cup finely crushed corn tortilla chips
1 egg, beaten
¼ cup salsa
⅓ cup shredded pepper Jack cheese
Pinch salt
Freshly ground black pepper
1 pound ground turkey
1 tablespoon olive oil
1 teaspoon paprika

Directions:
1. **Preparing the Ingredients.** In a medium bowl, combine the tortilla chips, egg, salsa, cheese, salt, and pepper, and mix well.
   Add the turkey and mix gently but thoroughly with clean hands.
   Form the meat mixture into patties about ½ inch thick. Make an indentation in the center of each patty with your thumb so the burgers don't puff up while cooking.
   Brush the patties on both sides with the olive oil and sprinkle with paprika.
2. **Air Frying.** Put in the Foodi SmartLid basket, lock the air fryer lid and Grill for 14 to 16 minutes or until the meat registers at least 165°F.

PER SERVING: CALORIES: 354; FAT: 21G; PROTEIN:36G; FIBER:2G

Air Fryer Turkey Breast

PREP: 5 MINUTES • COOK TIME: 60 MINUTES • TOTAL: 65 MINUTES
SERVES: 6

Ingredients
Pepper and salt
1 oven-ready turkey breast
Turkey seasonings of choice

Directions:
1. **Preparing the Ingredients.** Preheat the Foodi SmartLid to 350 degrees.
   Season turkey with pepper, salt, and other desired seasonings.
   Place turkey in Foodi SmartLid basket.
2. **Air Frying.** Lock the air fryer lid. Set temperature to 350°F, and set time to 60 minutes. Cook 60 minutes. The meat should be at 165 degrees when done.
   Allow to rest 10-15 minutes before slicing. Enjoy!

PER SERVING: CALORIES: 212; FAT: 12G; PROTEIN:24G; SUGAR:0G

Cheese Stuffed Chicken

PREP: 5 MINUTES • COOK TIME: 30 MINUTES •
TOTAL: 35 MINUTES
SERVES: 4

Ingredients

1 tablespoon creole seasoning
1 tablespoon olive oil
1 teaspoon garlic powder
1 teaspoon onion powder
4 chicken breasts, butterflied and pounded
4 slices Colby cheese
4 slices pepper jack cheese

Directions:
1. **Preparing the Ingredients.** Preheat the Foodi SmartLid to 390°F.
   Place the grill pan accessory in the Foodi SmartLid.
   Create the dry rub by mixing in a bowl the creole seasoning, garlic powder, and onion powder. Season with salt and pepper if desired.
   Rub the seasoning on to the chicken.
   Place the chicken on a working surface and place a slice each of pepper jack and Colby cheese.
   Fold the chicken and secure the edges with toothpicks.
   Brush chicken with olive oil.
2. **Air Frying.** Lock the air fryer lid. Grill for 30 minutes and make sure to flip the meat every 10 minutes.

PER SERVING: CALORIES: 27; FAT: 45.9G; PROTEIN:73.1G; SUGAR:0G

Orange Curried Chicken Stir-Fry

PREP: 10 MINUTES • COOK TIME: 18 MINUTES •
TOTAL: 28 MINUTES
SERVES: 4

Ingredients

¾ pound boneless, skinless chicken thighs, cut into 1-inch pieces
1 yellow bell pepper, cut into 1½-inch pieces
1 small red onion, sliced
Olive oil for misting
¼ cup chicken stock
2 tablespoons honey
¼ cup orange juice
1 tablespoon cornstarch
3 to 3 teaspoons curry powder

Directions:
1. **Preparing the Ingredients.** Put the chicken thighs, pepper, and red onion in the Foodi SmartLid basket and mist with olive oil.
2. **Air Frying.** Lock the air fryer lid. Cook for 12 to 14 minutes or until the chicken is cooked to 165°F, shaking the basket halfway through cooking time.
   Remove the chicken and vegetables from the Foodi SmartLid basket and set aside.
   In a 6-inch metal bowl, combine the stock, honey, orange juice, cornstarch, and curry powder, and mix well. Add the chicken and vegetables, stir, and put the bowl in the basket.
   Return the basket to the Foodi SmartLid and cook for 2 minutes. Remove and stir, then cook for 2 to 3 minutes or until the sauce is thickened and bubbly.

PER SERVING: CALORIES: 230; FAT: 7G; PROTEIN:26G; FIBER:2G

Mustard Chicken Tenders

PREP: 5 MINUTES • COOK TIME: 20 MINUTES • TOTAL: 25 MINUTES
SERVES: 4

Ingredients
½ C. coconut flour
1 tbsp. spicy brown mustard
2 beaten eggs
1 pound of chicken tenders

Directions:
1. **Preparing the Ingredients.** Season tenders with pepper and salt.
   Place a thin layer of mustard onto tenders and then dredge in flour and dip in egg.
2. **Air Frying.** Add to the Foodi SmartLid, lock the air fryer lid, set temperature to 390°F, and set time to 20 minutes.

PER SERVING: CALORIES: 403; FAT: 20G; PROTEIN:22G; SUGAR:4G

Chicken Pot Pie with Coconut Milk

PREP: 5 MINUTES • COOK TIME: 30 MINUTES • TOTAL: 40 MINUTES
SERVES: 8

Ingredients
¼ small onion, chopped
½ cup broccoli, chopped
¾ cup coconut milk
1 cup chicken broth
1/3 cup coconut flour
1-pound ground chicken
2 cloves of garlic, minced
2 tablespoons butter
4 ½ tablespoons butter, melted
4 eggs
Salt and pepper to taste

Directions:
1. **Preparing the Ingredients.** Preheat the Foodi SmartLid for 5 minutes.
   Place 2 tablespoons butter, broccoli, onion, garlic, coconut milk, chicken broth, and ground chicken in a baking dish that will fit in the Foodi SmartLid. Season with salt and pepper to taste.
   In a mixing bowl, combine the butter, coconut flour, and eggs.
   Sprinkle evenly the top of the chicken and broccoli mixture with the coconut flour dough.
   Place the dish in the Foodi SmartLid.
2. **Air Frying.** Lock the air fryer lid. Cook for 30 minutes at 325°F.

PER SERVING: CALORIES: 366; FAT: 29.5G; PROTEIN:21.8G; SUGAR:4G

Chicken Nuggets

PREP: 10 MINUTES • COOK TIME: 20 MINUTES • TOTAL: 30 MINUTES

SERVES: 4

Ingredients
1 pound boneless, skinless chicken breasts
Chicken seasoning or rub
Salt
Pepper
2 eggs
6 tablespoons bread crumbs
2 tablespoons panko bread crumbs
Cooking oil

Directions:
1. **Preparing the Ingredients.** Cut the chicken breasts into 1-inch pieces.
   In a large bowl, combine the chicken pieces with chicken seasoning, salt, and pepper to taste.
   In a small bowl, beat the eggs. In another bowl, combine the bread crumbs and panko.
   Dip the chicken pieces in the eggs and then the bread crumbs.
   Place the nuggets in the Foodi SmartLid. Do not overcrowd the basket. Cook in batches. Spray the nuggets with cooking oil.
2. **Air Frying.** Lock the air fryer lid. Cook for 4 minutes. Open the Foodi SmartLid and shake the basket. Cook for an additional 4 minutes. Remove the cooked nuggets from the Foodi SmartLid, then repeat for the remaining chicken nuggets. Cool before serving.

PER SERVING: CALORIES: 206; FAT: 5G; PROTEIN:31G; FIBER:1G

Cheesy Chicken Fritters
PREP: 5 MINUTES • COOK TIME: 20 MINUTES • TOTAL: 25 MINUTES
SERVES: 17 FRITTERS

Ingredients
Chicken Fritters:
½ tsp. salt
1/8 tsp. pepper
1 ½ tbsp. fresh dill
1 1/3 C. shredded mozzarella cheese
1/3 C. coconut flour
1/3 C. vegan mayo
2 eggs
1 ½ pounds chicken breasts
Garlic Dip:
1/8 tsp. pepper
¼ tsp. salt
½ tbsp. lemon juice
1 pressed garlic cloves
1/3 C. vegan mayo

Directions:
1. **Preparing the Ingredients.** Slice chicken breasts into 1/3" pieces and place in a bowl. Add all remaining fritter ingredients to the bowl and stir well. Cover and chill 2 hours or overnight.
   Ensure your Foodi SmartLid is preheated to 350 degrees. Spray basket with a bit of olive oil.
2. **Air Frying.** Add marinated chicken to Foodi SmartLid. Lock the air fryer lid, set temperature to 350°F, and set time to 20 minutes and cook 20 minutes, making sure to turn halfway through cooking process. To make the dipping sauce, combine all the dip ingredients until smooth.

PER SERVING: CALORIES: 467; FAT: 27G; PROTEIN:21G; SUGAR:3G

Chicken BBQ with Sweet And Sour Sauce

PREP: 5 MINUTES • COOK TIME: 40 MINUTES • TOTAL: 45 MINUTES
SERVES: 6

Ingredients

¼ cup minced garlic
¼ cup tomato paste
¾ cup minced onion
¾ cup sugar
1 cup soy sauce
1 cup water
1 cup white vinegar
6 chicken drumsticks
Salt and pepper to taste

Directions:

1. **Preparing the Ingredients.** Place all Ingredients in a Ziploc bag
    Allow to marinate for at least 2 hours in the fridge.
    Preheat the Foodi SmartLid to 390°F.
    Place the grill pan accessory in the Foodi SmartLid.
2. **Air Frying.** Lock the air fryer lid. Grill the chicken for 40 minutes.
    Flip the chicken every 10 minutes for even grilling.
    Meanwhile, pour the marinade in a saucepan and heat over medium flame until the sauce thickens.
    Before serving the chicken, brush with the glaze.

PER SERVING: CALORIES: 4607; FAT: 19.7G; PROTEIN:27.8G; SUGAR:3G

Crusted Chicken Tenders

PREP: 5 MINUTES • COOK TIME: 15 MINUTES • TOTAL: 20 MINUTES
SERVES: 3

Ingredients

½ cup all-purpose flour
2 eggs, beaten
½ cup seasoned breadcrumbs
Salt and freshly ground black pepper, to taste
2 tablespoons olive oil
¾ pound chicken tenders

Directions:

1. **Preparing the Ingredients.** In a bowl, place the flour.
    In a second bowl, place the eggs.
    In a third bowl, mix together breadcrumbs, salt, black pepper and oil.
    Coat the chicken tenders in the flour,
    Then dip into the eggs and finally coat with the breadcrumbs mixture evenly.
2. **Air Frying.** Preheat the Foodi SmartLid to 330 degrees F. Arrange the chicken tenderloins in Foodi SmartLid basket. Lock the air fryer lid. Cook for about 10 minutes. Now, set the Foodi SmartLid to 390 degrees F.
    Cook for about 5 minutes further.

Air Fryer Chicken Parmesan

PREP: 5 MINUTES • COOK TIME: 9 MINUTES • TOTAL: 20 MINUTES
SERVES: 4

Ingredients
½ C. keto marinara
6 tbsp. mozzarella cheese
1 tbsp. melted ghee
2 tbsp. grated parmesan cheese
6 tbsp. gluten-free seasoned breadcrumbs
1   8-ounce chicken breasts

Directions:
1. **Preparing the Ingredients.** Ensure Foodi SmartLid is preheated to 360 degrees. Spray the basket with olive oil.
   Mix parmesan cheese and breadcrumbs together. Melt ghee.
   Brush melted ghee onto the chicken and dip into breadcrumb mixture.
   Place coated chicken in the Foodi SmartLid and top with olive oil.
2. **Air Frying.** Lock the air fryer lid. Set temperature to 360°F, and set time to 6 minutes. Cook 2 breasts for 6 minutes and top each breast with a tablespoon of sauce and 1½ tablespoons of mozzarella cheese. Cook another 3 minutes to melt cheese. Keep cooked pieces warm as you repeat the process with remaining breasts.

PER SERVING: CALORIES: 251; FAT: 10G; PROTEIN:31G; SUGAR:0G

Chicken BBQ Recipe from Peru

PREP: 5 MINUTES • COOK TIME: 40 MINUTES • TOTAL: 45 MINUTES
SERVES: 4

Ingredients
½ teaspoon dried oregano
1 teaspoon paprika
1/3 cup soy sauce
2 ½ pounds chicken, quartered
2 tablespoons fresh lime juice
2 teaspoons ground cumin
5 cloves of garlic, minced

Directions:
1. **Preparing the Ingredients.** Place all Ingredients in a Ziploc bag and shake to mix everything.
   Allow to marinate for at least 2 hours in the fridge.
   Preheat the Foodi SmartLid to 390°F.
   Place the grill pan accessory in the Foodi SmartLid.
2. **Air Frying.** Lock the air fryer lid. Grill the chicken for 40 minutes making sure to flip the chicken every 10 minutes for even grilling.

PER SERVING: CALORIES: 377; FAT: 11.8G; PROTEIN:59.7G; SUGAR:0G

Ricotta and Parsley Stuffed Turkey Breasts

PREP: 5 MINUTES • COOK TIME: 25 MINUTES • TOTAL: 30 MINUTES
SERVES: 4

Ingredients
1 turkey breast, quartered
1 cup Ricotta cheese
1/4 cup fresh Italian parsley, chopped
1 teaspoon garlic powder
1/2 teaspoon cumin powder
1 egg, beaten
1 teaspoon paprika
Salt and ground black pepper, to taste
Crushed tortilla chips
1 ½ tablespoons extra-virgin olive oil

Directions:

1. **Preparing the Ingredients.** Firstly, flatten out each piece of turkey breast with a rolling pin. Prepare three mixing bowls.
   In a shallow bowl, combine Ricotta cheese with the parsley, garlic powder, and cumin powder.
   Place the Ricotta/parsley mixture in the middle of each piece. Repeat with the remaining pieces of the turkey breast and roll them up.
   In another shallow bowl, whisk the egg together with paprika. In the third shallow bowl, combine the salt, pepper, and crushed tortilla chips.
   Dip each roll in the whisked egg, then, roll them over the tortilla chips mixture. Transfer prepared rolls to the Foodi SmartLid basket. Drizzle olive oil over all.
2. **Air Frying.** Lock the air fryer lid. Cook at 350 degrees F for 25 minutes, working in batches. Serve warm, garnished with some extra parsley, if desired.

Cheesy Turkey-Rice with Broccoli

PREP: 5 MINUTES • COOK TIME: 40 MINUTES • TOTAL: 45 MINUTES
SERVES: 4

Ingredients
1 cup cooked, chopped turkey meat
1 tablespoon and 1-1/2 teaspoons butter, melted
1/2 (10 ounce) package frozen broccoli, thawed
1/2 (7 ounce) package whole wheat crackers, crushed
1/2 cup shredded Cheddar cheese
1/2 cup uncooked white rice

Directions:

1. **Preparing the Ingredients.** Bring to a boil 2 cups of water in a saucepan. Stir in rice and simmer for 20 minutes. Turn off fire and set aside.
   Lightly grease baking pan of Foodi SmartLid with cooking spray. Mix in cooked rice, cheese, broccoli, and turkey. Toss well to mix.
   Mix well melted butter and crushed crackers in a small bowl. Evenly spread on top of rice.
2. **Air Frying.** Lock the air fryer lid. For 20 minutes, cook on 360°F until tops are lightly browned.
   Serve and enjoy.

PER SERVING: CALORIES: 269; FAT: 11.8G; PROTEIN:17G; SUGAR:0G

Jerk Chicken Wings

PREP: 10 MINUTES • COOK TIME: 16 MINUTES • TOTAL: 26 MINUTES
SERVES: 6

Ingredients
1 tsp. salt
½ C. red wine vinegar
5 tbsp. lime juice
4 chopped scallions
1 tbsp. grated ginger
2 tbsp. brown sugar
1 tbsp. chopped thyme
1 tsp. white pepper
1 tsp. cayenne pepper
1 tsp. cinnamon
1 tbsp. allspice
1 Habanero pepper (seeds/ribs removed and chopped finely)
6 chopped garlic cloves
2 tbsp. low-sodium soy sauce
2 tbsp. olive oil
4 pounds of chicken wings

Directions:
1. **Preparing the Ingredients.** Combine all ingredients except wings in a bowl. Pour into a gallon bag and add chicken wings. Chill 2-24 hours to marinate.
Ensure your Foodi SmartLid is preheated to 390 degrees.
Place chicken wings into a strainer to drain excess liquids.
2. **Air Frying.** Pour half of the wings into your Foodi SmartLid. Lock the air fryer lid. Set temperature to 390°F, and set time to 16 minutes and cook 14-16 minutes, making sure to shake halfway through the cooking process.
Remove and repeat the process with remaining wings.

PER SERVING: CALORIES: 374; FAT: 14G; PROTEIN:33G; SUGAR:4G

Pork Recipes

Pork Shoulder Chops With Soy Sauce, Maple Syrup, And Carrots

PREP: 5 MINUTES • PRESSURE: 40 MINUTES • BROIL: 7 MINUTES • TOTAL: 52 MINUTES • PRESSURE LEVEL: HIGH • RELEASE: NATURAL
SERVES 6

Ingredients

1 tablespoon bacon fat
3 pounds bone-in pork shoulder chops, each ½ to ¾ inch thick
6 medium carrots
3 medium garlic cloves
⅓ cup soy sauce
⅓ cup maple syrup
⅓ cup chicken broth
½ teaspoon ground black pepper

Directions

1. **Preparing the Ingredients**. Melt the bacon fat in an Foodi SmartLid, turned to the sauté function. Add about half the chops and brown well, turning once, about 5 minutes. Transfer these to a large bowl and brown the remaining chops.
   Stir the carrots and garlic into the pot; cook for 1 minute, constantly stirring. Pour in the soy sauce, maple syrup, and broth, stirring to dissolve the maple syrup and to get up any browned bits on the bottom of the pot. Stir in the pepper. Return the shoulder chops and their juices to the pot. Stir to coat them in the sauce.
2. **High pressure for 40 minutes**. Lock the pressure cooking lid on the Foodi SmartLid and then cook for 40 minutes. To get 40-minutes cook time, press "Pressure" button and use the Time Adjustment button to adjust the cook time to 40 minutes.
3. **Pressure Release.** Let the pressure to come down naturally for at least 14 to 16 minutes, then quick release any pressure left in the pot.
4. **Finish the dish**. Close Air Fryer Lid and select Broil, set time to 7 minutes. Transfer the chops, carrots, and garlic cloves to a large serving bowl. Skim the fat off the sauce and ladle it over the servings.

Panko-Breaded Pork Chops

PREP: 5 MINUTES • COOK TIME: 12 MINUTES • TOTAL: 17 MINUTES
SERVES: 6

Ingredients
5 (3½- to 5-ounce) pork chops (bone-in or boneless)
Seasoning salt
Pepper
¼ cup all-purpose flour
2 tablespoons panko bread crumbs
Cooking oil

Directions:
1. **Preparing the Ingredients.** Season the pork chops with the seasoning salt and pepper to taste.
   Sprinkle the flour on both sides of the pork chops, then coat both sides with panko bread crumbs.
   Place the pork chops in the Foodi SmartLid. Stacking them is okay.
2. **Air Frying.** Spray the pork chops with cooking oil. Lock the air fryer lid. Cook for 6 minutes.
   Open the Foodi SmartLid and flip the pork chops. Cook for an additional 6 minutes
   Cool before serving.
   Typically, bone-in pork chops are juicier than boneless. If you prefer really juicy pork chops, use bone-in.

PER SERVING: CALORIES: 246; FAT: 13G; PROTEIN:26G; FIBER:0G

Apricot Glazed Pork Tenderloins

PREP: 5 MINUTES • COOK TIME: 30 MINUTES • TOTAL: 35 MINUTES
SERVES: 3

Ingredients
1 teaspoon salt
1/2 teaspoon pepper
1-lb pork tenderloin
2 tablespoons minced fresh rosemary or 1 tablespoon dried rosemary, crushed
2 tablespoons olive oil, divided
1 garlic cloves, minced

Apricot Glaze Ingredients
1 cup apricot preserves
1 garlic cloves, minced
4 tablespoons lemon juice

Directions:
1. **Preparing the Ingredients.** Mix well pepper, salt, garlic, oil, and rosemary. Brush all over pork. If needed cut pork crosswise in half to fit in Foodi SmartLid. Lightly grease baking pan of Foodi SmartLid with cooking spray. Add pork.
2. **Air Frying.** Lock the air fryer lid. For 3 minutes per side, brown pork in a preheated 390°F Foodi SmartLid.
   Meanwhile, mix well all glaze Ingredients in a small bowl. Baste pork every 5 minutes.
   Cook for 20 minutes at 330°F.
   Serve and enjoy.

PER SERVING: CALORIES: 281; FAT: 9G; PROTEIN:23G; FIBER:0G

Pulled Pork

PREP: 5 MINUTES • PRESSURE: 80 MINUTES • BROIL: 7 MINUTES • TOTAL: 92 MINUTES • PRESSURE LEVEL: HIGH • RELEASE: NATURAL
SERVES 8

Ingredients

2 tablespoons smoked paprika
2 tablespoons packed dark brown sugar
1 tablespoon ground cumin
2 teaspoons ground black pepper
½ tablespoon dry mustard
1 teaspoon ground coriander
1 teaspoon dried thyme
1 teaspoon onion powder
1 teaspoon salt
½ teaspoon garlic powder
½ teaspoon ground cloves
½ teaspoon ground cinnamon
One 4- to 4½-pound bone-in skinless pork shoulder, preferably pork butt
Up to 1½ cups light-colored beer, preferably a pale ale or amber lager

Directions

1. **Preparing the Ingredients**. Mix the smoked paprika, brown sugar, cumin, pepper, mustard, coriander, thyme, onion powder, salt, garlic powder, cloves, and cinnamon in a small bowl. Massage the mixture all over the pork.
   Set the pork in the Foodi SmartLid. Pour 1cup beer into the electric cooker without knocking the spices off the meat.
2. **High pressure for 80 minutes**. Lock the pressure cooking lid on the Foodi SmartLid and then cook for 80 minutes. To get 80-minutes cook time, press "Pressure" button and use the Time Adjustment button to adjust the cook time to 80 minutes.
3. **Pressure Release**. Let its pressure fall to normal naturally, 25 to 35 minutes.
4. **Finish the dish.** Close Air Fryer Lid and select Broil, set time to 7 minutes.
   Transfer the meat to a large cutting board. Let stand for 5 minutes. Use a spoon to skim as much fat off the sauce in the pot as possible.
   Set the "Saute" function. Bring the sauce to a simmer, stirring occasionally; continue boiling the sauce, often stirring, until reduced by half, 7 to 10 minutes.
   Use two forks to shred the meat off the bones; discard the bones and any attached cartilage. Pull any large chunks of meat apart with the forks and stir the meat back into the simmering sauce to reheat.
   Serve and Enjoy

Barbecue Flavored Pork Ribs

PREP: 5 MINUTES • COOK TIME: 15 MINUTES • TOTAL: 25 MINUTES
SERVES: 6

Ingredients
¼ cup honey, divided
¾ cup BBQ sauce
2 tablespoons tomato ketchup
1 tablespoon Worcestershire sauce
1 tablespoon soy sauce
½ teaspoon garlic powder
Freshly ground white pepper, to taste
1¾ pound pork ribs

Directions:
1. **Preparing the Ingredients.** In a large bowl, mix together 3 tablespoons of honey and remaining ingredients except pork ribs.
   Refrigerate to marinate for about 20 minutes.
   Preheat the Foodi SmartLid to 355 degrees F.
   Place the ribs in an Foodi SmartLid basket.
2. **Air Frying.** Lock the air fryer lid. Cook for about 13 minutes.
   Remove the ribs from the Foodi SmartLid and coat with remaining honey.
   Serve hot.

Rustic Pork Ribs

PREP: 5 MINUTES • COOK TIME: 15 MINUTES • TOTAL: 25 MINUTES
SERVES: 4

Ingredients
1 rack of pork ribs
3 tablespoons dry red wine
1 tablespoon soy sauce
1/2 teaspoon dried thyme
1/2 teaspoon onion powder
1/2 teaspoon garlic powder
1/2 teaspoon ground black pepper
1 teaspoon smoke salt
1 tablespoon cornstarch
1/2 teaspoon olive oil

Directions:
1. **Preparing the Ingredients.** Begin by preheating your Foodi SmartLid to 390 degrees F. Place all ingredients in a mixing bowl and let them marinate at least 1 hour.
2. **Air Frying.** Lock the air fryer lid. Cook the marinated ribs approximately 25 minutes at 390 degrees F.
   Serve hot.

Fried Pork Quesadilla

PREP: 10 MINUTES • COOK TIME: 12 MINUTES • TOTAL: 22 MINUTES
SERVES: 2

Ingredients

Two 6-inch corn or flour tortilla shells
1 medium-sized pork shoulder, approximately 4 ounces, sliced
½ medium-sized white onion, sliced
½ medium-sized red pepper, sliced
½ medium sized green pepper, sliced
½ medium sized yellow pepper, sliced
¼ cup of shredded pepper-jack cheese
¼ cup of shredded mozzarella cheese

Directions:

1. **Preparing the Ingredients.** Preheat the Foodi SmartLid to 350 degrees. Close Air Fryer Lid and select Broil, set time to 20 minutes. Grill the pork, onion, and peppers in foil in the same pan, allowing the moisture from the vegetables and the juice from the pork mingle together. After 20 minutes, remove pork and vegetables in foil. While they're cooling, sprinkle half the shredded cheese over one of the tortillas, then cover with the pieces of pork, onions, and peppers, and then layer on the rest of the shredded cheese. Top with the second tortilla. Place directly on hot surface of the Foodi SmartLid basket.
2. **Air Frying.** Lock the air fryer lid. Set the Foodi SmartLid timer for 6 minutes. After 6 minutes, when the Foodi SmartLid shuts off, flip the tortillas onto the other side with a spatula; the cheese should be melted enough that it won't fall apart, but be careful anyway not to spill any toppings!
Reset the Foodi SmartLid to 350 degrees for another 6 minutes.
After 6 minutes, when the Foodi SmartLid shuts off, the tortillas should be browned and crisp, and the pork, onion, peppers and cheese will be crispy and hot and delicious. Remove with tongs and let sit on a serving plate to cool for a few minutes before slicing.

Keto Parmesan Crusted Pork Chops

PREP: 10 MINUTES • COOK TIME: 15 MINUTES • TOTAL: 25 MINUTES
SERVES: 8

Ingredients
3 tbsp. grated parmesan cheese
1 C. pork rind crumbs
2 beaten eggs
¼ tsp. chili powder
½ tsp. onion powder
1 tsp. smoked paprika
¼ tsp. pepper
½ tsp. salt
4-6 thick boneless pork chops

Directions:
1. **Preparing the Ingredients.** Ensure your Foodi SmartLid is preheated to 400 degrees.
   With pepper and salt, season both sides of pork chops.
   In a food processor, pulse pork rinds into crumbs. Mix crumbs with other seasonings.
   Beat eggs and add to another bowl.
   Dip pork chops into eggs then into pork rind crumb mixture.
2. **Air Frying.** Spray down Foodi SmartLid with olive oil and add pork chops to the basket. Lock the air fryer lid.
   Set temperature to 400°F, and set time to 15 minutes.

PER SERVING: CALORIES: 422; FAT: 19G; PROTEIN:38G; SUGAR:2G

Pork Wonton Wonderful

PREP: 10 MINUTES • COOK TIME: 25 MINUTES • TOTAL: 35 MINUTES
SERVES: 3

Ingredients
8 wanton wrappers (Leasa brand works great, though any will do)
4 ounces of raw minced pork
1 medium-sized green apple
1 cup of water, for wetting the wanton wrappers
1 tablespoon of vegetable oil
½ tablespoon of oyster sauce
1 tablespoon of soy sauce
Large pinch of ground white pepper

Directions:
1. **Preparing the Ingredients.** Cover the basket of the Foodi SmartLid with a lining of tin foil, leaving the edges uncovered to allow air to circulate through the basket. Preheat the Foodi SmartLid to 350 degrees.
   In a small mixing bowl, combine the oyster sauce, soy sauce, and white pepper, then add in the minced pork and stir thoroughly. Cover and set in the fridge to marinate for at least 15 minutes. Core the apple, and slice into small cubes – smaller than bite-sized chunks.
   Add the apples to the marinating meat mixture, and combine thoroughly. Spread the wonton wrappers, and fill each with a large spoonful of the filling. Wrap the wontons into triangles, so that the wrappers fully cover the filling, and seal with a drop of the water.
   Coat each filled and wrapped wonton thoroughly with the vegetable oil, to help ensure a nice crispy fry. Place the wontons on the foil-lined air-fryer basket.

2. **Air Frying.** Lock the air fryer lid. Set the Foodi SmartLid timer to 25 minutes. Halfway through cooking time, shake the handle of the Foodi SmartLid basket vigorously to jostle the wontons and ensure even frying. After 25 minutes, when the Foodi SmartLid shuts off, the wontons will be crispy golden-brown on the outside and juicy and delicious on the inside. Serve directly from the Foodi SmartLid basket and enjoy while hot.

Tuscan Pork Chops

PREP: 10 MINUTES • COOK TIME: 10 MINUTES • TOTAL: 20 MINUTES
SERVES: 4

Ingredients
1/4 cup all-purpose flour
1 teaspoon salt
3/4 teaspoons seasoned pepper
4 (1-inch-thick) boneless pork chops
1 tablespoon olive oil
3 to 4 garlic cloves
1/3 cup balsamic vinegar
1/3 cup chicken broth
3 plum tomatoes, seeded and diced
1 tablespoons capers

Directions:

1. **Preparing the Ingredients.** Combine flour, salt, and pepper Press pork chops into flour mixture on both sides until evenly covered.

2. **Air Frying.** Lock the air fryer lid. Cook in your Foodi SmartLid at 360 degrees for 14 minutes, flipping half way through. While the pork chops cook, warm olive oil in a medium skillet. Add garlic and sauté for 1 minute; then mix in vinegar and chicken broth. Add capers and tomatoes and turn to high heat. Bring the sauce to a boil, stirring regularly, then add pork chops, cooking for one minute. Remove from heat and cover for about 5 minutes to allow the pork to absorb some of the sauce; serve hot.

PER SERVING: CALORIES: 349; FAT: 23G; PROTEIN:20G; FIBER:1.5G

Pork Loin With Apples

PREP: 5 MINUTES • PRESSURE: 30 MINUTES • TOTAL: 42 MINUTES • PRESSURE LEVEL: HIGH • RELEASE: QUICK
SERVES 6-8

Ingredients

2 tablespoons unsalted butter
One 3-pound boneless pork loin roast
1 large red onion, halved and thinly sliced
2 medium tart green apples, such as Granny Smith, peeled, cored, and thinly sliced
4 fresh thyme sprigs
2 bay leaves
½ cup moderately sweet white wine, such as Riesling
¼ cup chicken broth
½ teaspoon salt
½ teaspoon ground black pepper

Directions

1. **Preparing the Ingredients**. Melt the butter in the Foodi SmartLid, set on the "Sauté" function. Add the pork loin and brown it on all sides, turning occasionally, about 8 minutes in all. Transfer to a large plate.
Add the onion to the pot; cook, often stirring, until softened, about 3 minutes. Stir in the apple, thyme, and bay leaves. Pour in the wine and scrape up any browned bits on the bottom of the pot. Pour in the broth; stir in the salt and pepper. Nestle the pork loin into this apple mixture; pour any juices from the plate into the pot.
2. **High pressure for 30 minutes**. Lock the pressure cooking lid on the Foodi SmartLid and then cook for 30 minutes. To get 30-minutes cook time, press "Pressure" button and adjust the time.
3. **Pressure Release**. Use the quick-release method to bring the pot's pressure to normal.
4. **Finish the dish**. Close Air Fryer Lid and select Broil, set time to 7 minutes. Transfer the pork to a cutting board; let stand for 5 minutes while you dish the sauce into serving bowls or onto a serving platter. Slice the loin into ½-inch-thick rounds and lay these over the sauce.

Crispy Breaded Pork Chops

PREP: 10 MINUTES • COOK TIME: 15 MINUTES •
TOTAL: 25 MINUTES
SERVES: 8

Ingredients
1/8 tsp. pepper
¼ tsp. chili powder
½ tsp. onion powder
½ tsp. garlic powder
1 ¼ tsp. sweet paprika
2 tbsp. grated parmesan cheese
1/3 C. crushed cornflake crumbs
½ C. panko breadcrumbs
1 beaten egg
6 center-cut boneless pork chops

Directions:
1. **Preparing the Ingredients**. Ensure that your Foodi SmartLid is preheated to 400 degrees. Spray the basket with olive oil. With ½ teaspoon salt and pepper, season both sides of pork chops. Combine ¾ teaspoon salt with pepper, chili powder, onion powder, garlic powder, paprika, cornflake crumbs, panko breadcrumbs and parmesan cheese. Beat egg in another bowl. Dip pork chops into the egg and then crumb mixture. Add pork chops to Foodi SmartLid and spritz with olive oil.
2. **Air Frying**. Close Air Fryer Lid. Set temperature to 400°F, and set time to 12 minutes. Cook 12 minutes, making sure to flip over halfway through cooking process. Only add 3 chops in at a time and repeat the process with remaining pork chops.

PER SERVING: CALORIES: 378; FAT: 13G; PROTEIN:33G; SUGAR:1G

Crispy Roast Garlic-Salt Pork

PREP: 5 MINUTES • COOK TIME: 45 MINUTES •
TOTAL: 50 MINUTES
SERVES: 4

Ingredients
1 teaspoon Chinese five spice powder
1 teaspoon white pepper
2 pounds pork belly
2 teaspoons garlic salt

Directions:
1. **Preparing the Ingredients.** Preheat the Foodi SmartLid to 390°F.
   Mix all the spices in a bowl to create the dry rub.
   Score the skin of the pork belly with a knife and season the entire pork with the spice rub.
2. **Air Frying.** Place in the Foodi SmartLid basket, close Air Fryer Lid and cook for 40 to 45 minutes until the skin is crispy.
   Chop before serving.

PER SERVING: CALORIES: 785; FAT:80.7G; PROTEIN:14.2G; FIBER:0G

Peanut Satay Pork

PREP: 5 MINUTES • COOK TIME: 12 MINUTES • TOTAL: 17 MINUTES
SERVES: 5

Ingredients
11 Ozs Pork Fillet, sliced into bite sized strips
4 Cloves Garlic, crushed
1 Tsp Ginger Powder
2 Tsps Chili Paste
2 Tbsps Sweet Soy Sauce (Kecap Manis)
2 Tbsps Vegetable Oil
1 Shallot, finely chopped
1 Tsp Ground Coriander
3/4 Cup Coconut Milk
1/3 Cup Peanuts, ground

Directions:

1. **Preparing the Ingredients.** Mix half of the garlic in a dish with the ginger, a tablespoon of sweet soy sauce, and a tablespoon of the oil. Combine the meat into the mixture and leave to marinate for 15 minutes
Preheat the Foodi SmartLid to 390 degrees
2. **Air Frying.** Place the marinated meat into the Foodi SmartLid. Close the Air Fryer Lid, set the timer to 12 minutes and roast the meat until brown and done. Turn once while roasting
In the meantime, make the peanut sauce by heating the remaining tablespoon of oil in a saucepan and gently sauté the shallot with the garlic. Add the coriander and fry until fragrant
Mix the coconut milk and the peanuts with the chili paste and remaining soy sauce with the shallot mixture and gently boil for 5 minutes, while stirring
Drizzle over the cooked meat and serve with rice

Pork Tenderloin And Coconut Rice

PREP: 5 MINUTES • PRESSURE: 15 MINUTES • TOTAL: 27 MINUTES • PRESSURE LEVEL: HIGH • RELEASE: QUICK
SERVES 4

Ingredients
2 tablespoons peanut oil
1 pound pork tenderloin, cut into 4 pieces
1 small leek, white and pale green parts only, halved lengthwise, washed and thinly sliced
One 4½-ounce can chopped mild green chiles (about ½ cup)
1 teaspoon dried thyme
1 teaspoon ground cumin
½ teaspoon ground coriander
¼ teaspoon salt
¼ teaspoon ground black pepper
One 15-ounce can black beans, drained and rinsed (about 1¾ cups)
1 cup chicken broth
1 cup regular or low-fat canned coconut milk
1 cup white long-grain rice, such as white basmati rice
2 tablespoons packed light brown sugar

Directions

1. **Preparing the Ingredients.** Heat the oil in the Foodi SmartLid turned to the "Sauté" function. Add the pork tenderloin pieces; brown on all sides, occasionally turning, about 6 minutes. Transfer to a plate.
Add the leek and chiles; cook, often stirring, until the leek softens, about 2 minutes. Stir in the thyme, cumin, coriander, salt, and pepper; cook until aromatic, less than half a minute. Stir in the beans, broth, coconut milk, rice, and brown sugar until the brown sugar dissolves.
Nestle the pieces of pork in the sauce, submerging the meat and rice as much as

possible in the liquid; pour any juices from the meat's plate into the cooker.

2. **High pressure for 15 minutes**. Lock the pressure cooking lid on the Foodi SmartLid and then cook for 15 minutes. To get 15-minutes cook time, press "Pressure" Button and then adjust the time.

3. **Pressure Release**. Use the quick-release method to bring the pot's pressure back to normal but do not open the cooker.
Set the pot aside for 10 minutes to steam the rice.

4. **Finish the dish**. Close air fryer lid and select Broil, set time to 7 minutes.
Transfer the pork pieces to four serving plates; spoon the rice and beans around them

Ginger, Garlic And Pork Dumplings

PREP: 10 MINUTES • COOK TIME: 15 MINUTES • TOTAL: 25 MINUTES
SERVES: 8

Ingredients
¼ teaspoon crushed red pepper
½ teaspoon sugar
1 tablespoon chopped fresh ginger
1 tablespoon chopped garlic
1 teaspoon canola oil
1 teaspoon toasted sesame oil
18 dumpling wrappers
2 tablespoons rice vinegar
2 teaspoons soy sauce
4 cups bok choy, chopped
4 ounces ground pork

Directions:

1. **Preparing the Ingredients.** Heat oil in a skillet and sauté the ginger and garlic until fragrant. Stir in the ground pork and cook for 5 minutes.
Stir in the bok choy and crushed red pepper. Season with salt and pepper to taste. Allow to cool.
Place the meat mixture in the middle of the dumpling wrappers. Fold the wrappers to seal the meat mixture in.
Place the bok choy in the grill pan.

2. **Air Frying**. Close air fryer lid. Cook the dumplings in the Foodi SmartLid at 330°F for 15 minutes.
Meanwhile, prepare the dipping sauce by combining the remaining Ingredients in a bowl.

PER SERVING: CALORIES: 137; FAT: 5G; PROTEIN:7G

Pork Tenderloin with Braised Apples

PREP: 5 MINUTES • PRESSURE: 45 MINUTES • TOTAL: 50 MINUTES • PRESSURE LEVEL: HIGH • RELEASE: QUICK
SERVES 4

Ingredients.

For The Brine (optional)
½ cup Diamond Crystal kosher salt, or ¼ cup fine table salt
¼ cup granulated sugar
2 cups very hot tap water
2 cups ice water

For The Pork And Apples
1 (1-pound) pork tenderloin, trimmed of silver skin and halved crosswise
Kosher salt, for salting and seasoning
2 tablespoons unsalted butter
1 cup thinly sliced onion
1 medium Granny Smith apple, or another tart apple, peeled and cut into ¼-inch slices
¾ cup apple juice, cider, or hard cider
½ cup low-sodium chicken broth
2 tablespoons heavy (whipping) cream
1 teaspoon Dijon mustard, plus additional as needed

Directions

1. **Preparing the Ingredients.**

    -To make the brine (if using)

    In a large stainless steel or glass bowl, dissolve the salt and sugar in hot water; then stir in the ice water. Submerge the pork in the brine, and refrigerate for 2 to 3 hours. Drain and pat dry.

    -To make the pork and apples

    If you choose not to brine the pork, sprinkle it liberally with kosher salt.

    Set to "Sauté" heat the butter just until it stops foaming. Add the pork halves, browning on all sides, about 4 minutes total. Transfer to a plate or rack, and set aside.

    Add the onion slices to the cooker, and cook, stirring, for 2 to 3 minutes, or until they just start to brown. Add the apple slices, and cook for 1 minute. Add the apple juice, and scrape the browned bits from the bottom of the pot. Bring to a simmer, and cook for 2 to 3 minutes, or until the juice has reduced by about one-third. Add the chicken broth, and return the pork tenderloin to the cooker, placing the pieces on top of the apples and onions.

2. **High pressure for 45 minutes**. Lock the pressure cooking lid on the Foodi SmartLid and then cook for 45 minutes. To get 45-minutes cook time, press "Pressure" button and use the adjust button to adjust the cook time to 45 minutes.

3. **Pressure Release**. Use the quick-release method.

4. **Finish the dish.** Close air fryer lid. Discard the bay leaves. Select AIR FRY, set temperature to 375°F, and set time to 10 minutes. Check after 5 minutes, cooking for an additional 5 minutes if dish needs more browning.

Transfer the pork to a plate or rack, and tent it with aluminum foil while you finish the sauce.

Turn the Foodi SmartLid to "Sauté", simmer for about 6 minutes, or until the liquid is reduced by about half. Stir in the heavy cream and mustard, and taste, adding kosher salt or more mustard as needed.

Slice the pork into ¾-inch pieces, and place on a serving platter. Spoon the apples, onions, and sauce over the pork, and serve.

PER SERVING: CALORIES: 321; FAT: 13G; SODIUM: 754MG; CARBOHYDRATES: 21G; FIBER: 2G; PROTEIN: 32G

Caramelized Pork Shoulder

PREP: 10 MINUTES • COOK TIME: 20 MINUTES • TOTAL: 30 MINUTES
SERVES: 8

Ingredients
1/3 cup soy sauce
2 tablespoons sugar
1 tablespoon honey
2 pound pork shoulder, cut into 1½-inch thick slices

Directions:

1 **Preparing the Ingredients.** In a bowl, mix together all ingredients except pork. Add pork and coat with marinade generously.
Cover and refrigerate o marinate for about 2-8 hours.
Preheat the Foodi SmartLid to 335 degrees F.

2 **Air Frying.** Place the pork in an Foodi SmartLid basket. Close the air fryer lid. Cook for about 10 minutes.
Now, set the Foodi SmartLid to 390 degrees F. Cook for about 10 minutes

Curry Pork Roast in Coconut Sauce

PREP: 10 MINUTES • COOK TIME: 60 MINUTES • TOTAL: 70 MINUTES
SERVES: 6

Ingredients
½ teaspoon curry powder
½ teaspoon ground turmeric powder
1 can unsweetened coconut milk
1 tablespoons sugar
2 tablespoons fish sauce
2 tablespoons soy sauce
3 pounds pork shoulder
Salt and pepper to taste

Directions:

1. **Preparing the Ingredients.** Place all Ingredients in bowl and allow the meat to marinate in the fridge for at least 2 hours. Preheat the Foodi SmartLid to 390°F.
Place the grill pan accessory in the Foodi SmartLid.
2. **Air Frying.** Close air fryer lid. Grill the meat for 20 minutes making sure to flip the pork every 10 minutes for even grilling and cook in batches.
Meanwhile, pour the marinade in a saucepan and allow to simmer for 10 minutes until the sauce thickens.
Baste the pork with the sauce before serving.

PER SERVING: CALORIES: 688; FAT: 52G; PROTEIN:17G

Chinese Salt and Pepper Pork Chop Stir-fry

PREP: 10 MINUTES • COOK TIME: 15 MINUTES • TOTAL: 25 MINUTES
SERVES: 4

Ingredients
Pork Chops:
Olive oil
¾ C. almond flour
¼ tsp. pepper
½ tsp. salt
1 egg white
Pork Chops
Stir-fry:
¼ tsp. pepper
1 tsp. sea salt
2 tbsp. olive oil
2 sliced scallions
2 sliced jalapeno peppers

Directions:
1. **Preparing the Ingredients.** Coat the Foodi SmartLid basket with olive oil. Whisk pepper, salt, and egg white together till foamy.
Cut pork chops into pieces, leaving just a bit on bones. Pat dry.
Add pieces of pork to egg white mixture, coating well. Let sit for marinade 20 minutes.
Put marinated chops into a large bowl and add almond flour. Dredge and shake off excess and place into Foodi SmartLid.
2. **Air Frying.** Close air fryer lid. Set temperature to 360°F, and set time to 12 minutes. Cook 12 minutes at 360 degrees. Turn up the heat to 400 degrees and cook another 6 minutes till pork chops are nice and crisp.
To make stir-fry, remove jalapeno seeds and chop up. Chop scallions and mix with jalapeno pieces.
Heat a skillet with olive oil. Stir-fry pepper, salt, scallions, and jalapenos 60

seconds. Then add fried pork pieces to skills and toss with scallion mixture. Stir-fry 1-2 minutes till well coated and hot.

PER SERVING: CALORIES: 294; FAT: 17G; PROTEIN:36G; SUGAR:4G

Roasted Pork Tenderloin
PREP: 5 MINUTES • COOK TIME: 1 HOUR • TOTAL: 65 MINUTES
SERVES: 4

Ingredients
1 (3-pound) pork tenderloin
2 tablespoons extra-virgin olive oil
2 garlic cloves, minced
1 teaspoon dried basil
1 teaspoon dried oregano
1 teaspoon dried thyme
Salt
Pepper

Directions:
1. **Preparing the Ingredients.** Drizzle the pork tenderloin with the olive oil.
   Rub the garlic, basil, oregano, thyme, and salt and pepper to taste all over the tenderloin.
2. **Air Frying.** Place the tenderloin in the Foodi SmartLid. Close air fryer lid. Cook for 45 minutes.
   Use a meat thermometer to test for doneness
   Open the Foodi SmartLid and flip the pork tenderloin. Cook for an additional 15 minutes.
   Remove the cooked pork from the Foodi SmartLid and allow it to rest for 10 minutes before cutting.

PER SERVING: CALORIES: 283; FAT: 10G; PROTEIN:48G

Garlic Putter Pork Chops

PREP: 10 MINUTES • COOK TIME: 7 MINUTES • TOTAL: 17 MINUTES
SERVES: 4

Ingredients
2 tsp. parsley
2 tsp. grated garlic cloves
1 tbsp. coconut oil
1 tbsp. coconut butter
4 pork chops

Directions:
1. **Preparing the Ingredients.** Ensure your Foodi SmartLid is preheated to 350 degrees.
   Mix butter, coconut oil, and all seasoning together. Then rub seasoning mixture over all sides of pork chops. Place in foil, seal, and chill for 1 hour.
   Remove pork chops from foil and place into Foodi SmartLid.
2. **Air Frying.** Close air fryer lid. Set temperature to 350°F, and set time to 7 minutes. Cook 7 minutes on one side and 8 minutes on the other.
   Drizzle with olive oil and serve alongside a green salad.

PER SERVING: CALORIES: 526; FAT: 23G; PROTEIN:41G; SUGAR:4G

Fried Pork with Sweet and Sour Glaze

PREP: 5 MINUTES • COOK TIME: 30 MINUTES • TOTAL: 35 MINUTES
SERVES: 4

Ingredients
¼ cup rice wine vinegar
¼ teaspoon Chinese five spice powder
1 cup potato starch
1 green onion, chopped
2 large eggs, beaten
2 pounds pork chops cut into chunks
2 tablespoons cornstarch + 3 tablespoons water
5 tablespoons brown sugar
Salt and pepper to taste

Directions:
1. **Preparing the Ingredients.** Preheat the Foodi SmartLid to 390°F.
   Season pork chops with salt and pepper to taste.
   Dip the pork chops in egg. Set aside.
   In a bowl, combine the potato starch and Chinese five spice powder.
   Dredge the pork chops in the flour mixture.
2. **Air Frying.** Close air fryer lid. Place in the double layer rack and cook for 30 minutes. Meanwhile, place the vinegar and brown sugar in a saucepan. Season with salt and pepper to taste. Stir in the cornstarch slurry and allow to simmer until thick.
   Serve the pork chops with the sauce and garnish with green onions.

PER SERVING: CALORIES: 420; FAT: 11.8G; PROTEIN:69.2G

Pork Cutlet Rolls

PREP: 10 MINUTES • COOK TIME: 15 MINUTES • TOTAL: 25 MINUTES
SERVES: 4

Ingredients
4 Pork Cutlets
4 Sundried Tomatoes in oil
2 Tbsps Parsley, finely chopped
1 Green Onion, finely chopped
Black Pepper to taste
2 Tsps Paprika
1/2 Tbsp Olive Oil
* String for Rolled Meat

Directions:
1. **Preparing the Ingredients.** Preheat the Foodi SmartLid to 390 degrees
   Finely chop the tomatoes and mix with the parsley and green onion. Add salt and pepper to taste
   Spread out the cutlets and coat them with the tomato mixture. Roll up the cutlets and secure intact with the string
   Rub the rolls with salt, pepper, and paprika powder and thinly coat them with olive oil
2. **Air Frying.** Put the cutlet rolls in the Foodi SmartLid tray, close air fryer lid and cook for 15 minutes. Roast until nicely brown and done.
   Serve with tomato sauce.

Oregano-Paprika on Breaded Pork

PREP: 10 MINUTES • COOK TIME: 30 MINUTES • TOTAL: 40 MINUTES
SERVES: 4

Ingredients
¼ cup water
¼ teaspoon dry mustard
½ teaspoon black pepper
½ teaspoon cayenne pepper
½ teaspoon garlic powder
½ teaspoon salt
1 cup panko breadcrumbs
1 egg, beaten
2 teaspoons oregano
4 lean pork chops
4 teaspoons paprika

Directions:
1. **Preparing the Ingredients.** Preheat the Foodi SmartLid to 390°F.
   Pat dry the pork chops.
   In a mixing bowl, combine the egg and water. Then set aside.
   In another bowl, combine the rest of the Ingredients.
   Dip the pork chops in the egg mixture and dredge in the flour mixture.
2. **Air Frying.** Place in the Foodi SmartLid basket, close air fryer lid and cook for 25 to 30 minutes until golden.

PER SERVING: CALORIES: 364; FAT: 20.2G; PROTEIN:42.9G

Bacon Wrapped Pork Tenderloin

PREP: 5 MINUTES • COOK TIME: 15 MINUTES •
TOTAL: 20 MINUTES
SERVES: 4

Ingredients
Pork:
1-2 tbsp. Dijon mustard
3-4 strips of bacon
1 pork tenderloin
Apple Gravy:
½ - 1 tsp. Dijon mustard
1 tbsp. almond flour
2 tbsp. ghee
1 chopped onion
2-3 Granny Smith apples
1 C. vegetable broth

Directions:
1. **Preparing the Ingredients.** Spread Dijon mustard all over tenderloin and wrap meat with strips of bacon.
2. **Air Frying**. Place into the Foodi SmartLid, close air fryer lid, set temperature to 360°F, and set time to 15 minutes and cook 10-15 minutes at 360 degrees. Use a meat thermometer to check for doneness.
To make sauce, heat ghee in a pan and add shallots. Cook 1-2 minutes.
Then add apples, cooking 3-5 minutes until softened.
Add flour and ghee to make a roux. Add broth and mustard, stirring well to combine.
When sauce starts to bubble, add 1 cup of sautéed apples, cooking till sauce thickens.
Once pork tenderloin I cook, allow to sit 5-10 minutes to rest before slicing.
Serve topped with apple gravy. Devour!

PER SERVING: CALORIES: 552; FAT: 25G; PROTEIN:29G; SUGAR:6G

Dijon Garlic Pork Tenderloin

PREP: 5 MINUTES • COOK TIME: 10 MINUTES •
TOTAL: 15 MINUTES
SERVES: 6

Ingredients
1 C. breadcrumbs
Pinch of cayenne pepper
3 crushed garlic cloves
2 tbsp. ground ginger
2 tbsp. Dijon mustard
2 tbsp. raw honey
4 tbsp. water
2 tsp. salt
1 pound pork tenderloin, sliced into 1-inch rounds

Directions:

1. **Preparing the Ingredients.** With pepper and salt, season all sides of tenderloin. Combine cayenne pepper, garlic, ginger, mustard, honey, and water until smooth. Dip pork rounds into honey mixture and then into breadcrumbs, ensuring they all get coated well.
Place coated pork rounds into your Foodi SmartLid.
2. **Air Frying**. Close air fryer lid, set temperature to 400°F, and set time to 10 minutes. Cook 10 minutes at 400 degrees. Flip and then cook an additional 5 minutes until golden in color.

PER SERVING: CALORIES: 423; FAT: 18G; PROTEIN:31G; SUGAR:3G

Pork Neck with Salad

PREP: 10 MINUTES • COOK TIME: 12 MINUTES • TOTAL: 22 MINUTES
SERVES: 2

Ingredients

For Pork:
1 tablespoon soy sauce
1 tablespoon fish sauce
½ tablespoon oyster sauce
½ pound pork neck
For Salad:
1 ripe tomato, sliced tickly
8-10 Thai shallots, sliced
1 scallion, chopped
1 bunch fresh basil leaves
1 bunch fresh cilantro leaves
For Dressing:
3 tablespoons fish sauce
2 tablespoons olive oil
1 teaspoon apple cider vinegar
1 tablespoon palm sugar
2 bird eye chili
1 tablespoon garlic, minced

Directions:

1. **Preparing the Ingredients.** For pork in a bowl, mix together all ingredients except pork.
   Add pork neck and coat with marinade evenly. Refrigerate for about 2-3 hours.
   Preheat the Foodi SmartLid to 340 degrees F.
2. **Air Frying.** Place the pork neck onto a grill pan. Close air fryer lid and cook for about 12 minutes.
   Meanwhile in a large salad bowl, mix together all salad ingredients.
   In a bowl, add all dressing ingredients and beat till well combined.
   Remove pork neck from Foodi SmartLid and cut into desired slices.
   Place pork slices over salad.

Cajun Pork Steaks

PREP: 5 MINUTES • COOK TIME: 20 MINUTES • TOTAL: 25 MINUTES
SERVES: 6

Ingredients

4-6 pork steaks
BBQ sauce:
Cajun seasoning
1 tbsp. vinegar
1 tsp. low-sodium soy sauce
½ C. brown sugar
½ C. vegan ketchup

Directions:

1. **Preparing the Ingredients.** Ensure your Foodi SmartLid is preheated to 290 degrees.
   Sprinkle pork steaks with Cajun seasoning.
   Combine remaining ingredients and brush onto steaks. Add coated steaks to Foodi SmartLid.
2. **Air Frying.** Close air fryer lid. Set temperature to 290°F, and set time to 20 minutes. Cook 15-20 minutes till just browned.

PER SERVING: CALORIES: 209; FAT: 11G; PROTEIN:28G; SUGAR:2G

Wonton Taco Cups

PREP: 5 MINUTES • COOK TIME: 10 MINUTES • TOTAL: 15 MINUTES
SERVES: 8

Ingredients
1/2 pound ground pork, browned and drained
1/2 pound ground beef, browned and drained
1 envelope taco seasoning
1 (10-ounce) can tomatoes with chilies, diced and drained
1 bell pepper, seeded and chopped
32 wonton wrappers
1 cup Cheddar cheese, shredded

Directions:
1. **Preparing the Ingredients.** Combine the pork, beef, taco seasoning, diced tomatoes, and bell pepper; mix well.
   Line all the muffin cups with wonton wrappers. Spritz with a nonstick cooking oil. Divide the beef filling among wrappers; top with the shredded cheese.
2. **Air Frying.** Close air fryer lid. Bake at 370 degrees F for about 10 minutes or until heated through.

Cajun Sweet-Sour Grilled Pork

PREP: 5 MINUTES • COOK TIME: 12 MINUTES • TOTAL: 17 MINUTES
SERVES: 3

Ingredients
¼ cup brown sugar
1/4 cup cider vinegar
1-lb pork loin, sliced into 1-inch cubes
2 tablespoons Cajun seasoning
3 tablespoons brown sugar

Directions:
1. **Preparing the Ingredients.** In a shallow dish, mix well pork loin, 3 tablespoons brown sugar, and Cajun seasoning. Toss well to coat. Marinate in the ref for 3 hours. In a medium bowl mix well, brown sugar and vinegar for basting.
   Thread pork pieces in skewers. Baste with sauce and place on skewer rack in Foodi SmartLid.
2. **Air Frying.** Close air fryer lid, for 12 minutes, cook on 360°F. Halfway through cooking time, turnover skewers and baste with sauce. If needed, cook in batches. Serve and enjoy.

PER SERVING: CALORIES: 428; FAT: 16.7G; PROTEIN:39G; SUGAR:2G

Chinese Braised Pork Belly

PREP: 5 MINUTES • COOK TIME: 20 MINUTES • TOTAL: 25 MINUTES
SERVES: 8

Ingredients
1 lb Pork Belly, sliced
1 Tbsp Oyster Sauce
1 Tbsp Sugar
2 Red Fermented Bean Curds
1 Tbsp Red Fermented Bean Curd Paste
1 Tbsp Cooking Wine
1/2 Tbsp Soy Sauce
1 Tsp Sesame Oil
1 Cup All Purpose Flour

Directions:
1. **Preparing the Ingredients.** Preheat the Foodi SmartLid to 390 degrees.
   In a small bowl, mix all ingredients together and rub the pork thoroughly with this mixture
   Set aside to marinate for at least 30 minutes or preferably overnight for the flavors to permeate the meat
   Coat each marinated pork belly slice in flour and place in the Foodi SmartLid tray
2. **Air Frying.** Close air fryer lid. Cook for 15 to 20 minutes until crispy and tender.

Air Fryer Sweet and Sour Pork

PREP: 10 MINUTES • COOK TIME: 12 MINUTES • TOTAL: 22 MINUTES
SERVES: 6

Ingredients
3 tbsp. olive oil
1/16 tsp. Chinese Five Spice
¼ tsp. pepper
½ tsp. sea salt
1 tsp. pure sesame oil
2 eggs
1 C. almond flour
2 pounds pork, sliced into chunks
Sweet and Sour Sauce:
¼ tsp. sea salt
½ tsp. garlic powder
1 tbsp. low-sodium soy sauce
½ C. rice vinegar
5 tbsp. tomato paste
1/8 tsp. water
½ C. sweetener of choice

Directions:

1. **Preparing the Ingredients.** To make the dipping sauce, whisk all sauce ingredients together over medium heat, stirring 5 minutes. Simmer uncovered 5 minutes till thickened.
   Meanwhile, combine almond flour, five spice, pepper, and salt.
   In another bowl, mix eggs with sesame oil. Dredge pork in flour mixture and then in egg mixture. Shake any excess off before adding to Foodi SmartLid basket.
2. **Air Frying.** Close air fryer lid. Set temperature to 340°F, and set time to 12 minutes.
   Serve with sweet and sour dipping sauce!

PER SERVING: CALORIES: 371; FAT: 17G; PROTEIN:27G; SUGAR:1G

Pork Loin with Potatoes

PREP: 10 MINUTES • COOK TIME: 25 MINUTES • TOTAL: 35 MINUTES
SERVES: 2

Ingredients
2 pounds pork loin
1 teaspoon fresh parsley, chopped
2 large red potatoes, chopped
½ teaspoon garlic powder
½ teaspoon red pepper flakes, crushed
Salt and freshly ground black pepper, to taste

Directions:

1. **Preparing the Ingredients.** In a large bowl, add all ingredients except glaze and toss to coat well. Preheat the Foodi SmartLid to 325 degrees F. Place the loin in the Foodi SmartLid basket.
Arrange the potatoes around pork loin.
2. **Air Frying.** Close air fryer lid. Cook for about 25 minutes.

Fried Pork Scotch Egg
PREP: 10 MINUTES • COOK TIME: 25 MINUTES • TOTAL: 35 MINUTES
SERVES: 2

Ingredients
3 soft-boiled eggs, peeled
8 ounces of raw minced pork, or sausage outside the casings
2 teaspoons of ground rosemary
2 teaspoons of garlic powder
Pinch of salt and pepper
2 raw eggs
1 cup of breadcrumbs (Panko, but other brands are fine, or home-made bread crumbs work too)

Directions:

1. **Preparing the Ingredients.** Cover the basket of the Foodi SmartLid with a lining of tin foil, leaving the edges uncovered to allow air to circulate through the basket. Preheat the Foodi SmartLid to 350 degrees.
In a mixing bowl, combine the raw pork with the rosemary, garlic powder, salt and pepper. This will probably be easiest to do with your masher or bare hands (though make sure to wash thoroughly after handling raw meat!); combine until all the spices are evenly spread throughout the meat.
Divide the meat mixture into three equal portions in the mixing bowl, and form each into balls with your hands.
Lay a large sheet of plastic wrap on the countertop, and flatten one of the balls of meat on top of it, to form a wide, flat meat-circle.
Place one of the peeled soft-boiled eggs in the center of the meat-circle and then, using the ends of the plastic wrap, pull the

meat-circle so that it is fully covering and surrounding the soft-boiled egg.

Tighten and shape the plastic wrap covering the meat so that if forms a ball, and make sure not to squeeze too hard lest you squish the soft-boiled egg at the center of the ball! Set aside.

Repeat with the other two soft-boiled eggs and portions of meat-mixture.

In a separate mixing bowl, beat the two raw eggs until fluffy and until the yolks and whites are fully combined.

One by one, remove the plastic wrap and dunk the pork-covered balls into the raw egg, and then roll them in the bread crumbs, covering fully and generously. Place each of the bread-crumb covered meat-wrapped balls onto the foil-lined surface of the Foodi SmartLid. Three of them should fit nicely, without touching.

2. **Air Frying.** Close air fryer lid. Set the Foodi SmartLid timer to 25 minutes. About halfway through the cooking time, shake the handle of the air-fryer vigorously, so that the scotch eggs inside roll around and ensure full coverage. After 25 minutes, the Foodi SmartLid will shut off and the scotch eggs should be perfect – the meat fully cooked, the egg-yolks still runny on the inside, and the outsides crispy and golden-brown. Using tongs, place them on serving plates, slice in half, and enjoy

Roasted Char Siew (Pork Butt)

PREP: 10 MINUTES • COOK TIME: 25 MINUTES • TOTAL: 35 MINUTES
SERVES: 6

Ingredients
1 strip of pork shoulder butt with a good amount of fat marbling
Marinade:
1 tsp. sesame oil
4 tbsp. raw honey
1 tsp. low-sodium dark soy sauce
1 tsp. light soy sauce
1 tbsp. rose wine
2 tbsp. Hoisin sauce

Directions:
1. **Preparing the Ingredients.** Combine all marinade ingredients together and add to Ziploc bag. Place pork in bag, making sure all sections of pork strip are engulfed in the marinade. Chill 3-24 hours.
Take out the strip 30 minutes before planning to cook and preheat your Foodi SmartLid to 350 degrees.
Place foil on small pan and brush with olive oil. Place marinated pork strip onto prepared pan.
2. **Air Frying.** Close air fryer lid.
Set temperature to 350°F, and set time to 20 minutes. Roast 20 minutes.
Glaze with marinade every 5-10 minutes. Remove strip and leave to cool a few minutes before slicing.

PER SERVING: CALORIES: 289; FAT: 13G; PROTEIN:33G; SUGAR:1G

Juicy Pork Ribs Ole

PREP: 10 MINUTES • COOK TIME: 25 MINUTES • TOTAL: 35 MINUTES
SERVES: 4

Ingredients
1 rack of pork ribs
1/2 cup low-fat milk
1 tablespoon envelope taco seasoning mix
1 can tomato sauce
1/2 teaspoon ground black pepper
1 teaspoon seasoned salt
1 tablespoon cornstarch
1 teaspoon canola oil

Directions:
1. **Preparing the Ingredients.** Place all ingredients in a mixing dish; let them marinate for 1 hour.
2. **Air Frying.** Close air fryer lid. Cook the marinated ribs approximately 25 minutes at 390 degrees F
Work with batches. Enjoy

Asian Pork Chops

PREP: 2 HOURS 10 MINUTES • COOK TIME: 15 MINUTES • TOTAL: 2 HOURS, 25 MINUTES
SERVES: 4

Ingredients
1/2 cup hoisin sauce
3 tablespoons cider vinegar
1 tablespoon Asian sweet chili sauce
1/4 teaspoon garlic powder
4 (1/2-inch-thick) boneless pork chops
1 teaspoon salt
1/2 teaspoon pepper

Directions:
1. **Preparing the Ingredients.** Stir together hoisin, chili sauce, garlic powder, and vinegar in a large mixing bowl. Separate 1/4 cup of this mixture, then add pork chops to the bowl and marinate in the fridge for 2 hours. Remove the pork chops and place them on a plate. Sprinkle each side of the pork chop evenly with salt and pepper.
2. **Air Frying.** Close air fryer lid. Cook at 360 degrees for 14 minutes, flipping half way through. Brush with reserved marinade and serve.

PER SERVING: CALORIES: 338; FAT: 21G; PROTEIN: 19G; FIBER: 1G

Teriyaki Pork Rolls

PREP: 10 MINUTES • COOK TIME: 8 MINUTES • TOTAL: 20 MINUTES
SERVES: 6

Ingredients
1 tsp. almond flour
4 tbsp. low-sodium soy sauce
4 tbsp. mirin
4 tbsp. brown sugar
Thumb-sized amount of ginger, chopped
Pork belly slices
Enoki mushrooms

Directions:
1. **Preparing the Ingredients.** Mix brown sugar, mirin, soy sauce, almond flour, and ginger together until brown sugar dissolves.
Take pork belly slices and wrap around a bundle of mushrooms. Brush each roll with teriyaki sauce. Chill half an hour.
Preheat your Foodi SmartLid to 350 degrees and add marinated pork rolls.
2. **Air Frying.** Close air fryer lid.
Set temperature to 350°F, and set time to 8 minutes.

PER SERVING: CALORIES: 412; FAT: 9G; PROTEIN:19G; SUGAR:4G

Ham and Cheese Rollups

PREP: 5 MINUTES • COOK TIME: 8 MINUTES • TOTAL: 15 MINUTES
SERVES: 12

Ingredients
2 tsp. raw honey
2 tsp. dried parsley
1 tbsp. poppy seeds
½ C. melted coconut oil
¼ C. spicy brown mustard
9 slices of provolone cheese
10 ounces of thinly sliced Black Forest Ham
1 tube of crescent rolls

Directions:
1. **Preparing the Ingredients.** Roll out dough into a rectangle. Spread 2-3 tablespoons of spicy mustard onto dough, then layer provolone cheese and ham slices.
Roll the filled dough up as tight as you can and slice into 12-15 pieces.
Melt coconut oil and mix with a pinch of salt and pepper, parsley, honey, and remaining mustard.
Brush mustard mixture over roll-ups and sprinkle with poppy seeds.
Grease Foodi SmartLid basket liberally with olive oil and add rollups.
2. **Air Frying.** Close air fryer lid.
Set temperature to 350°F, and set time to 8 minutes.
Serve!

PER SERVING: CALORIES: 289; FAT: 6G; PROTEIN:18G; SUGAR

Vietnamese Pork Chops

PREP: 10 MINUTES • COOK TIME: 7 MINUTES • TOTAL: 25 MINUTES
SERVES: 6

Ingredients
1 tbsp. olive oil
1 tbsp. fish sauce
1 tsp. low-sodium dark soy sauce
1 tsp. pepper
3 tbsp. lemongrass
1 tbsp. chopped shallot
1 tbsp. chopped garlic
1 tbsp. brown sugar
2 pork chops

Directions:
1. **Preparing the Ingredients.** Add pork chops to a bowl along with olive oil, fish sauce, soy sauce, pepper, lemongrass, shallot, garlic, and brown sugar. Marinade pork chops 2 hours.
Ensure your Foodi SmartLid is preheated to 400 degrees. Add pork chops to the basket.
2. **Air Frying.** Close air fryer lid. Set temperature to 400°F, and set time to 7 minutes. Cook making sure to flip after 5 minutes of cooking.
Serve alongside steamed cauliflower rice.

PER SERVING: CALORIES: 290; FAT: 15G; PROTEIN:30G; SUGAR:3G

Beef Recipes

Cheeseburger Egg Rolls

PREP: 10 MINUTES • COOK TIME: 7 MINUTES •
TOTAL: 17 MINUTES
SERVES: 6

Ingredients
6 egg roll wrappers
6 chopped dill pickle chips
1 tbsp. yellow mustard
3 tbsp. cream cheese
3 tbsp. shredded cheddar cheese
½ C. chopped onion
½ C. chopped bell pepper
¼ tsp. onion powder
¼ tsp. garlic powder
8 ounces of raw lean ground beef

Directions:
1. **Preparing the Ingredients.** In a skillet, add seasonings, beef, onion, and bell pepper. Stir and crumble beef till fully cooked, and vegetables are soft.
   Take skillet off the heat and add cream cheese, mustard, and cheddar cheese, stirring till melted.
   Pour beef mixture into a bowl and fold in pickles.
   Lay out egg wrappers and place 1/6th of beef mixture into each one. Moisten egg roll wrapper edges with water. Fold sides to the middle and seal with water.
   Repeat with all other egg rolls.
   Place rolls into Foodi SmartLid, one batch at a time.
2. **Air Frying.** Close air fryer lid. Set temperature to 392°F, and set time to 7 minutes.

PER SERVING: CALORIES: 153; FAT: 4G; PROTEIN:12G; SUGAR:3G

Brisket With Veggies

PREP: 10 MINUTES • PRESSURE: 60 MINUTES • BROIL: 8 MINUTES • TOTAL: 78 MINUTES • PRESSURE LEVEL: HIGH • RELEASE: QUICK
SERVES 6

Ingredients

2 tbs. olive oil
5 or 6 red potatoes
2 lb. or larger regular brisket, rinsed and patted dry
Fresh ground black pepper
3 tbs. heaping chopped garlic
1 lg. yellow onion
2 c. large chunks carrots
2-½ c. homemade beef broth, or make from Knorr Beef Base
3 tbs. Worcestershire Sauce
4 bay leaves
5 or 6 red potatoes
Granulated garlic
Knorr Demi-Glace sauce
½ c. dehydrated onion
2 stalks celery in 1" chunks

Directions

1. **Preparing the Ingredients.** Put the Foodi SmartLid on the sauté setting. Put in 1 tbs. (more if needed) of the oil and caramelize the onions. Once golden, remove from pot, put in a bowl, and set aside. But keep the Foodi SmartLid on the "Sauté" setting.
   Rub the freshly ground pepper on both sides of the brisket. Do the same with the granulated garlic. Add 1tbs. olive oil (or more) and only lightly sear the brisket on all sides.
   Add back the onions, garlic, Worcestershire sauce, bay leaves, dehydrated onion and beef broth.
2. **High pressure for 50 minutes.** Close the pressure cooking lid and the pressure valve and then cook for 50 minutes. To get 50-minutes cook time, press "Pressure" button and use the Time Adjustment button to adjust the cook time to 50 minutes.
   While the meat is cooking, peel and cut up all the veggies. When the meat is done, use the quick pressure release feature, and then remove the lid. Add all of the veggies, replace the lid and cook at high pressure for to 10 minutes. To get 10-minutes cook time, press "Steam" button
3. **Pressure Release.** When the time is up, turn the pot off, use the quick release again, and remove the lid.
4. **Finish the dish.** Close air fryer lid. Select BROIL, and set time to 8 minutes. Check after 5 minutes, cooking for an additional 3 minutes if dish needs more browning.
   Use a platter to remove the veggies and meat. Use the "Sauté" setting and bring the broth to a boil, then add the Knorr Demi-Glace mixing with a Wisk. Adjust seasonings as needed. Serve with Cole Slaw or other salad, homemade rolls or Italian garlic bread. Be sure to remove the bay leaves before serving.
   Serve and Enjoy

Juicy Cheeseburgers

PREP: 5 MINUTES • COOK TIME: 15 MINUTES • TOTAL: 20 MINUTES
SERVES: 4

Ingredients

1 pound 93% lean ground beef
1 teaspoon Worcestershire sauce
1 tablespoon burger seasoning
Salt
Pepper
Cooking oil
4 slices cheese
buns

Directions:

1. **Preparing the Ingredients**.
   In a large bowl, mix the ground beef, Worcestershire, burger seasoning, and salt and pepper to taste until well blended. Spray the Foodi SmartLid basket with cooking oil. You will need only a quick spritz. The burgers will produce oil as they cook. Shape the mixture into 4 patties. Place the burgers in the Foodi SmartLid. The burgers should fit without the need to stack, but stacking is okay if necessary.

2. **Air Frying**. Close air fryer lid. Cook for 8 minutes. Open the Foodi SmartLid and flip the burgers. Cook for an additional 3 to 4 minutes. Check the inside of the burgers to determine if they have finished cooking. You can stick a knife or fork in the center to examine the color.
   Top each burger with a slice of cheese. Cook for an additional minute, or until the cheese has melted. Serve on buns with any additional toppings of your choice.

PER SERVING: CALORIES: 566; FAT: 39G; PROTEIN:29G; FIBER:1G

Country Fried Steak

PREP: 5 MINUTES • COOK TIME: 12 MINUTES • TOTAL: 20 MINUTES
SERVES: 2

Ingredients

1 tsp. pepper
2 C. almond milk
2 tbsp. almond flour
6 ounces ground sausage meat
1 tsp. pepper
1 tsp. salt
1 tsp. garlic powder
1 tsp. onion powder
1 C. panko breadcrumbs
1 C. almond flour
3 beaten eggs
6 ounces sirloin steak, pounded till thin

Directions:

1. **Preparing the Ingredients**. Season panko breadcrumbs with spices.
   Dredge steak in flour, then egg, and then seasoned panko mixture.
   Place into Foodi SmartLid basket.

2. **Air Frying**. Close air fryer lid. Set temperature to 370°F, and set time to 12 minutes.
   To make sausage gravy, cook sausage and drain off fat, but reserve 2 tablespoons. Add flour to sausage and mix until incorporated. Gradually mix in milk over medium to high heat till it becomes thick. Season mixture with pepper and cook 3 minutes longer.
   Serve steak topped with gravy and enjoy!

PER SERVING: CALORIES: 395; FAT: 11G; PROTEIN:39G; SUGAR:5G

Beef Ribs

PREP: 10 MINUTES • PRESSURE: 60 MINUTES • BROIL: 10 MINUTES • TOTAL: 80 MINUTES • PRESSURE LEVEL: HIGH • RELEASE: NORMAL
SERVES 4-6

Ingredients

1 tablespoon sesame oil
2 cloves garlic, peeled and smashed
1" knob fresh ginger, peeled and finely chopped
1 pinch red pepper flakes
¼ cup rice vinegar (or white balsamic vinegar)
⅓ cup raw sugar
⅔ cup soy sauce
⅔ cup salt-free (home made) beef stock
4 pounds (2k) beef ribs (about 8), ask the butcher to saw or chop them in half
2 tablespoons cornstarch
1-2 tablespoons water

Directions

1. **Preparing the Ingredients**. Turn on the Foodi SmartLid to "Sauté" mode.
   Add sesame oil garlic, ginger and red pepper flakes and sauté for a minute.
   Then, de-glaze with vinegar, mix-in the sugar, soy sauce and beef stock - mix well. Add the ribs to the Foodi SmartLid coating them with the mixture.
2. **High pressure for 60 minutes**. Close and lock the pressure cooking lid of the Foodi SmartLid, cook at high pressure for 60 minutes. To get 60-minutes cook time, press "Pressure" button and use the Time Adjustment button to adjust the cook time to 60 minutes.
3. **Pressure Release**. Use the Natural release method (20 minutes).
4. **Finish the dish**. Remove the lid from the Foodi SmartLid. Close air fryer lid. Select BROIL, and set time to 10 minutes. Check after 6 minutes, cooking for an additional 4 minutes if dish needs more browning.

Make a slurry with the cornstarch and water and then mix into the rib cooking liquid in the Foodi SmartLid. "Sauté" the mixture until it reaches the desired consistency.
Serve and Enjoy

Per Serving Calories:
307.3; Carbohydrates: 8.6g; Fat: 10.7g; Fiber: 10.6g; Protein: 32.3g; Sodium: 1654.6mg; Cholesterol: 89.2g

Spicy Thai Beef Stir-Fry

PREP: 15 MINUTES • COOK TIME: 9 MINUTES • TOTAL: 24 MINUTES
SERVES: 4

Ingredients
1 pound sirloin steaks, thinly sliced
2 tablespoons lime juice, divided
⅓ cup crunchy peanut butter
½ cup beef broth
1 tablespoon olive oil
1½ cups broccoli florets
2 cloves garlic, sliced
1 to 2 red chile peppers, sliced

Directions:
1. **Preparing the Ingredients.** In a medium bowl, combine the steak with 1 tablespoon of the lime juice. Set aside.
Combine the peanut butter and beef broth in a small bowl and mix well. Drain the beef and add the juice from the bowl into the peanut butter mixture.
In a 6-inch metal bowl, combine the olive oil, steak, and broccoli.
2. **Air Frying.** Close air fryer lid. Cook for 3 to 4 minutes or until the steak is almost cooked and the broccoli is crisp and tender, shaking the basket once during cooking time.
Add the garlic, chile peppers, and the peanut butter mixture and stir.
Cook for 3 to 5 minutes or until the sauce is bubbling and the broccoli is tender.
Serve over hot rice.

PER SERVING: CALORIES: 387; FAT: 22G; PROTEIN:42G; FIBER:2G

Lamb Casserole

PREP: 15 MINUTES • PRESSURE: 35 MINUTES • AIR CRISP: 15 MINUTES • TOTAL: 65 MINUTES • PRESSURE LEVEL: HIGH • RELEASE: NORMAL
SERVES 6-8

Ingredients
1 pound of baby potatoes
1 pound rack of lamb
2 carrots
1 large onion
2 stalks of celery
1-2 teaspoons of salt depending on the salt content of the chicken stock
2 medium size tomatoes
2 cups of chicken stock
3-4 large cloves of garlic
2 teaspoon of cumin powder
2 teaspoon of Paprika
A pinch of dried rosemary
A pinch of dried oregano leaves
2 tablespoons of ketchup
3 tablespoons of sherry or red wine
A splash of beer if you have one in hand

Directions
1. **Preparing the Ingredients.** Dice the tomatoes, onion, and garlic, cut potatoes, and carrots, cut the rack of lamb into two halves. Put all the ingredients, in the Foodi SmartLid.
2. **High pressure for 35 minutes**. Lock the pressure cooking lid on the Foodi SmartLid and then cook for 35 minutes. To get 35-minutes cook time, press "Pressure" button and adjust the time.
3. **Pressure Release**. Use Natural-Release Method for 10 minutes, and then Quick-Release.
Remove the lid from the Foodi SmartLid. Close air fryer lid. Select AIR FRY, set temperature to 400°F, and set time to 15 minutes. Check after 10 minutes, cooking for an additional 5 minutes if dish needs more browning.

Serve and Enjoy

Per Serving Calories: 407.3; Carbohydrates: 6.6g; Fat: 11.7g; Fiber: 8.6g; Protein: 35.3g; Sodium: 1640.6mg; Cholesterol: 77.2

Barbecued Baby Back Ribs

PREP: 5 MINUTES • PRESSURE: 32 MINUTES • AIR CRISP: 15 MINUTES • TOTAL: 52 MINUTES • PRESSURE LEVEL: HIGH • RELEASE: NATURAL
SERVES 4

Ingredients

¼ cup canned tomato paste
2 tablespoons cider vinegar
1 tablespoon sweet paprika
½ tablespoon coriander seeds
½ tablespoon fennel seeds
1 teaspoon onion powder
1 teaspoon dried thyme
½ teaspoon ground allspice
½ teaspoon salt
½ teaspoon ground black pepper
¼ teaspoon celery seeds
One 4-pound rack baby back ribs, cut into 2 or 3 sections to fit in the cooker

Directions

1. **Preparing the Ingredients**. Whisk the tomato paste, vinegar, paprika, coriander and fennel seeds, onion powder, thyme, allspice, salt, pepper, and celery seeds with ¾ cup water in an electric Foodi SmartLid until the tomato paste dissolves. Add the ribs; toss to coat thoroughly and evenly in the sauce.
2. **High pressure for 32 minutes**. Lock the pressure cooking lid on the Foodi SmartLid and then cook for 32 minutes. To get 32-minutes cook time, press "Pressure" button and use the Time Adjustment button to adjust the cook time to 32 minutes.
3. **Pressure Release**. Let the pressure to come down naturally for at least 15 minutes, then quick release any pressure left in the pot.
4. **Finish the dish**. Remove the lid from the Foodi SmartLid. Close air fryer lid. Select AIR FRY, set temperature to 400°F, and set

time to 15 minutes. Check after 10 minutes, cooking for an additional 5 minutes if dish needs more browning.

5. Transfer the rib rack sections to a large rimmed baking sheet. Set the electric one to its browning function. Bring the sauce to a simmer. Cook, stirring occasionally, until the sauce has thickened, 3 to 5 minutes. Position the oven rack 4 to 6 inches from the broiler; heat the broiler. Brush a light coating of the sauce onto the ribs, then broil until glazed and hot, 6 to 8 minutes, turning once. Slice the racks between the bones to make individual ribs. Serve with the extra sauce on the side.

Sausage And Peppers

PREP: 5 MINUTES • PRESSURE: 10 MINUTES • AIR CRISP: 10 MINUTES • TOTAL: 25 MINUTES • PRESSURE LEVEL: HIGH • RELEASE: QUICK
SERVES 6

Ingredients

2 tablespoons olive oil
2½ pounds sweet Italian sausages in their casings
4 large red bell peppers, stemmed, seeded, and cut into strips
1 medium red onion, halved and thinly sliced
2 medium garlic cloves, slivered
1 cup red (sweet) vermouth
2 tablespoons balsamic vinegar
¼ teaspoon grated nutmeg

Directions

1. **Preparing the Ingredients.** Heat the oil in an Foodi SmartLid, turned to the sauté function. Prick the sausages with a fork, add them to the pot, and brown on all sides, about 6 minutes. Transfer to a large bowl.
   Add the peppers and onion; cook, stirring almost constantly, just until the pepper strips glisten, about 2 minutes. Add the garlic, cook a few seconds, and then stir in the vermouth, vinegar, and nutmeg.
   Nestle the sausages into the mixture.
2. **High pressure for 10 minutes.** Lock the pressure cooking lid on the Foodi SmartLid and Cook for 10 minutes. To get 10-minutes cook time, press the "Pressure" button and adjust the time.
3. **Pressure Release.** Use the quick-release method to bring the pot's pressure back to normal.
   Remove the lid from the Foodi SmartLid. Close air fryer lid. Select AIR FRY, set temperature to 390°F, and set time to 10 minutes. Check after 8 minutes, cooking

for an additional 2 minutes if dish needs more browning.

Stir well before serving.

Spicy Sausage And Chard Pasta Sauce

PREP: 5 MINUTES • PRESSURE: 6 MINUTES • BROIL: 5 MINUTES • TOTAL: 16 MINUTES • PRESSURE LEVEL: HIGH • RELEASE: QUICK
SERVES 6

Ingredients

2 tablespoons olive oil
1 medium red onion, chopped
Up to 3 small hot chiles, such as cherry peppers or Anaheim chiles, stemmed, seeded, and chopped
1 tablespoon minced garlic
1 pound mild Italian pork sausage meat, any casings removed
½ cup dry red wine, such as Syrah
½ cup canned tomato paste
¼ cup chicken broth
1 tablespoon dried basil
2 teaspoons dried oregano
4 cups stemmed and chopped Swiss chard

Directions

1. **Preparing the Ingredients**. Heat the oil in an Foodi SmartLid, turned to the sauté function.
   Add the onion and cook, often stirring, until softened, about 4 minutes. Add the chiles and garlic; cook until aromatic, stirring all the while, about 1 minute.
   Crumble in the sausage meat, breaking up any clumps with a wooden spoon. Stir until it loses its raw color. Stir in the wine, tomato paste, broth, basil, and oregano until the tomato paste dissolves. Add the chard and stir well.
2. **High pressure for 6 minutes**. Lock the pressure cooking lid onto the cooker, set the machine's timer to cook at high pressure for 6 minutes. To get 6-minutes cook time, press the "Pressure" button and use the Time Adjustment button to adjust the cook time to 6 minutes.

3. **Pressure Release**. Use the quick-release method to drop the pressure back to normal.
4. **Finish the dish**. Remove the lid from the Foodi SmartLid. Close air fryer lid. Select BROIL, and set time to 5 minutes. Check after 4 minutes, cooking for an additional 4 minutes if dish needs more browning. Stir well before serving.

Meat Lovers' Pizza
PREP: 10 MINUTES • COOK TIME: 12 MINUTES • TOTAL: 22 MINUTES
SERVES: 2

Ingredients
1 pre-prepared 7-inch pizza pie crust, defrosted if necessary.
1/3 cup of marinara sauce.
2 ounces of grilled steak, sliced into bite-sized pieces
2 ounces of salami, sliced fine
2 ounces of pepperoni, sliced fine
¼ cup of American cheese
¼ cup of shredded mozzarella cheese

Directions:

1. **Preparing the Ingredients.** Preheat the Foodi SmartLid to 350 degrees. Lay the pizza dough flat on a sheet of parchment paper or tin foil, cut large enough to hold the entire pie crust, but small enough that it will leave the edges of the air frying basket uncovered to allow for air circulation. Using a fork, stab the pizza dough several times across the surface – piercing the pie crust will allow air to circulate throughout the crust and ensure even cooking. With a deep soup spoon, ladle the marinara sauce onto the pizza dough, and spread evenly in expanding circles over the surface of the pie-crust. Be sure to leave at least ½ inch of bare dough around the edges, to ensure that extra-crispy crunchy first bite of the crust! Distribute the pieces of steak and the slices of salami and pepperoni evenly over the sauce-covered dough, then sprinkle the cheese in an even layer on top.
2. **Air Frying.** Set the Foodi SmartLid timer to 12 minutes, and place the pizza with

foil or paper on the fryer's basket surface. Again, be sure to leave the edges of the basket uncovered to allow for proper air circulation, and don't let your bare fingers touch the hot surface. Close air fryer lid. After 12 minutes, when the Foodi SmartLid shuts off, the cheese should be perfectly melted and lightly crisped, and the pie crust should be golden brown. Using a spatula – or two, if necessary, remove the pizza from the Foodi SmartLid basket and set on a serving plate. Wait a few minutes until the pie is cool enough to handle, then cut into slices and serve.

Chimichurri Skirt Steak

PREP: 10 MINUTES • COOK TIME: 8 MINUTES • TOTAL: 18 MINUTES
SERVES: 2

Ingredients
2 x 8 oz Skirt Steak
1 cup Finely Chopped Parsley
¼ cup Finely Chopped Mint
2 Tbsp Fresh Oregano (Washed & finely chopped)
3 Finely Chopped Cloves of Garlic
1 Tsp Red Pepper Flakes (Crushed)
1 Tbsp Ground Cumin
1 Tsp Cayenne Pepper
2 Tsp Smoked Paprika
1 Tsp Salt
¼ Tsp Pepper
¾ cup Oil
3 Tbsp Red Wine Vinegar

Directions:
1. **Preparing the Ingredients.** Throw all the ingredients in a bowl (besides the steak) and mix well.
   Put ¼ cup of the mixture in a plastic baggie with the steak and leave in the fridge overnight (2–24hrs).
2. **Air Frying.** Leave the bag out at room temperature for at least 30 min before popping into the Foodi SmartLid. Preheat for a minute or two to 390° F before cooking until med-rare (8–10 min).
   Put 2 Tbsp of the chimichurri mix on top of each steak before serving.

Ground Beef Stew

PREP: 5 MINUTES • PRESSURE: 5 MINUTES • AIR CRISP: 15 MINUTES • TOTAL: 25 MINUTES • PRESSURE LEVEL: HIGH • RELEASE: QUICK
SERVES 4

Ingredients

1 tablespoon olive oil
1½ pounds lean ground beef (about 93% lean)
1 large yellow onion, chopped
1 large sweet potato (about 1 pound), peeled and shredded through the large holes of a box grater
1 teaspoon ground cinnamon
1 teaspoon ground cumin
½ teaspoon dried sage
½ teaspoon dried oregano
½ teaspoon salt
½ teaspoon ground black pepper
2 tablespoons yellow cornmeal
2 tablespoons honey
2½ cups beef broth

Directions

1. **Preparing the Ingredients.** Heat the oil in the Foodi SmartLid turned to the Sauté function. Crumble in the ground beef; cook, stirring occasionally, until it loses its raw color and browns a bit, about 5 minutes. Add the onion; cook, often stirring, until softened, about 3 minutes.
   Stir in the sweet potato, cinnamon, cumin, sage, oregano, salt, and pepper. Cook for 1 minute, stirring constantly. Stir in the cornmeal and honey; cook for 1 minute, often stirring, to dissolve the cornmeal. Stir in the broth.
2. **High pressure for 5 minutes.** Lock the pressure cooking lid on the Foodi SmartLid and then cook for 5 minutes. To get 5-minutes cook time, press "Pressure" button and use the Time Adjustment button to adjust the cook time to 5 minutes.
3. **Pressure Release.** Use the quick-release method to drop the pot's pressure to normal.
4. **Finish the dish.** Remove the lid from the Foodi SmartLid. Close air fryer lid. Select AIR FRY, set temperature to 390°F, and set time to 20 minutes. Check after 15 minutes, cooking for an additional 15 minutes if dish needs more browning.
   Stir well and set aside, loosely covered, for 5 minutes before serving.

Creamy Burger & Potato Bake

PREP: 5 MINUTES • COOK TIME: 55 MINUTES • TOTAL: 60 MINUTES
SERVES: 3

Ingredients
salt to taste
freshly ground pepper, to taste
1/2 (10.75 ounce) can condensed cream of mushroom soup
1/2-pound lean ground beef
1-1/2 cups peeled and thinly sliced potatoes
1/2 cup shredded Cheddar cheese
1/4 cup chopped onion
1/4 cup and 2 tablespoons milk

Directions:

1. **Preparing the Ingredients.** Lightly grease baking pan of Foodi SmartLid with cooking spray. Add ground beef. For 10 minutes, cook on 360°F. Stir and crumble halfway through cooking time.
   Meanwhile, in a bowl, whisk well pepper, salt, milk, onion, and mushroom soup. Mix well.
   Drain fat off ground beef and transfer beef to a plate.
   In same Foodi SmartLid baking pan, layer ½ of potatoes on bottom, then ½ of soup mixture, and then ½ of beef. Repeat process.
   Cover pan with foil.
2. **Air Frying.** Close air fryer lid. Cook for 30 minutes. Remove foil and cook for another 15 minutes or until potatoes are tender. Serve and enjoy.

PER SERVING: CALORIES: 399; FAT: 26.9G; PROTEIN:22.1G

Lamb with Mexican Sauce

PREP: 10 MINUTES • PRESSURE: 45 MINUTES • AIR CRISP: 15 MINUTES • TOTAL: 70 MINUTES • PRESSURE LEVEL: HIGH • RELEASE: NORMAL
SERVES 3-4

Ingredients
3 lamb shoulder
1 Spanish onion
3 garlic cloves, minced
1 19 oz. can Old El Paso Enchilada sauce
2 Tbsp. oil
Salt to taste
Cilantro, chopped without the stems
Corn tortillas (3-4 per person)
Limes cut into 8ths
Black beans or refried beans
Chipotle-style rice

Directions

1. **Preparing the Ingredients.** Marinate lamb overnight in Old El Paso Enchilada sauce (mild, medium or hot).
   Turn on the Foodi SmartLid to "sauté" mode.
   Add oil. Put in the onions and cook until soft, add garlic and cook for 1 minute.
   Add the lamb and marinade wait until boil.
2. **High pressure for 45 minutes.** Lock the pressure cooking lid on the Foodi SmartLid and then cook for 45 minutes. To get 45-minutes cook time, press "Pressure" button and use the adjust button to adjust the cook time to 45 minutes.
3. **Pressure Release.** Let the pressure to come down naturally for at least 15 minutes, then quick release any pressure left in the pot.
4. **Finish the dish.** Remove the lid from the Foodi SmartLid. Close air fryer lid. Select AIR FRY, set temperature to 375°F, and set time to 15 minutes. Check after 10 minutes, cooking for an additional 5 minutes if dish needs more browning.

Cut the limes, heat the beans put the hot rice into a serving bowl.

Set the Lamb aside. Ladle a generous amount of sauce over it.

Heat up 3-4 corn tortillas.

Put the lamb mixture onto a soft warm corn tortilla, sprinkle on cilantro, then squeeze with lime juice.

Serve and Enjoy

Beefy And Cheesy Spanish Rice Casserole

PREP: 10 MINUTES • COOK TIME: 50 MINUTES • TOTAL: 60 MINUTES
SERVES: 3

Ingredients
2 tablespoons chopped green bell pepper
1 tablespoon chopped fresh cilantro
1/2-pound lean ground beef
1/2 cup water
1/2 teaspoon salt
1/2 teaspoon brown sugar
1/2 pinch ground black pepper
1/3 cup uncooked long grain rice
1/4 cup finely chopped onion
1/4 cup chile sauce
1/4 teaspoon ground cumin
1/4 teaspoon Worcestershire sauce
1/4 cup shredded Cheddar cheese
1/2 (14.5 ounce) can canned tomatoes

Directions:
1. **Preparing the Ingredients.** Lightly grease baking pan of Foodi SmartLid with cooking spray. Add ground beef.
2. **Air Frying.** Close air fryer lid. For 10 minutes, cook on 360°F. Halfway through cooking time, stir and crumble beef. Discard excess fat,
Stir in pepper, Worcestershire sauce, cumin, brown sugar, salt, chile sauce, rice, water, tomatoes, green bell pepper, and onion. Mix well. Cover pan with foil and cook for 25 minutes. Stirring occasionally. Give it one last good stir, press down firmly and sprinkle cheese on top.
Cook uncovered for 15 minutes at 390°F until tops are lightly browned.
Serve and enjoy with chopped cilantro.

PER SERVING: CALORIES: 346; FAT: 19.1G; PROTEIN:18.5G

Pulled BBQ Beef Sandwiches

PREP: 10 MINUTES • PRESSURE: 35 MINUTES • AIR CRISP: 15 MINUTES • TOTAL: 60 MINUTES • PRESSURE LEVEL: HIGH • RELEASE: NORMAL
SERVES 2-4

Ingredients

2 pounds – Beef of choice
2 cps – Water
4 cps – Finely shredded Cabbage (the secret ingredient and you'll never know it's in there.)
1/2 cup – Of your favorite BBQ Sauce
1 cup – Ketchup
1/3 cup – Worcestershire Sauce
1 tblsp – Horse Radish
1 tblsp – mustard

Directions

1. **Preparing the Ingredients**. Add and stir in ingredients to your Foodi SmartLid.
2. **High pressure for 35 minutes**. Lock the pressure Cooking lid on the Foodi SmartLid and then cook for 35 minutes. To get 35-minutes cook time, press "Pressure" button and adjust the time.
3. **Pressure Release**. Use natural release method.
4. **Finish the dish**. Remove the lid from the Foodi SmartLid. Close air fryer lid. Select AIR FRY, set temperature to 390°F, and set time to 15 minutes. Check after 10 minutes, cooking for an additional 5 minutes if dish needs more browning.
Set the beef aside. Set the Foodi SmartLid to a "Sauté" mode, Sauté the sauce until it reaches the desired consistency.
Serve and Enjoy.

Beef & veggie Spring Rolls

PREP: 5 MINUTES • **COOK TIME:** 12 MINUTES • **TOTAL:** 55 MINUTES
SERVES: 10

Ingredients
2-ounce Asian rice noodles
1 tablespoon sesame oil
7-ounce ground beef
1 small onion, chopped
3 garlic cloves, crushed
1 cup fresh mixed vegetables
1 teaspoon soy sauce
1 packet spring roll skins
2 tablespoons water
Olive oil, as required

Directions:
1. **Preparing the Ingredients.** Soak the noodles in warm water till soft.
   Drain and cut into small lengths. In a pan heat the oil and add the onion and garlic and sauté for about 4-5 minutes.
   Add beef and cook for about 4-5 minutes.
   Add vegetables and cook for about 5-7 minutes or till cooked through.
   Stir in soy sauce and remove from the heat.
   Immediately, stir in the noodles and keep aside till all the juices have been absorbed.
   Preheat the Foodi SmartLid to 350 degrees F. and preheat the oven to 350 degrees F also.
   Place the spring rolls skin onto a smooth surface.
   Add a line of the filling diagonally across.
   Fold the top point over the filling and then fold in both sides.
   On the final point brush it with water before rolling to seal.
   Brush the spring rolls with oil.
2. **Air Frying.** Arrange the rolls in batches in the Foodi SmartLid, close air fryer lid and Cook for about 8 minutes.
   Repeat with remaining rolls.

Now, place spring rolls onto a baking sheet.
Bake for about 6 minutes per side.

Lamb And Eggplant Pasta Casserole

PREP: 10 MINUTES • PRESSURE: 8 MINUTES • BROIL: 5 MINUTES • TOTAL: 18 MINUTES • PRESSURE LEVEL: HIGH • RELEASE: QUICK
SERVES 4

Ingredients

2 tablespoons olive oil
1 medium red onion, chopped
1 tablespoon minced garlic
1½ pounds lean ground lamb
One small eggplant (about ¾ pound), stemmed and diced
¾ cup dry red wine, such as Syrah
2¼ cups chicken broth
½ cup canned tomato paste
1 teaspoon ground cinnamon
½ tablespoon dried oregano
½ teaspoon dried dill
½ teaspoon salt
½ teaspoon ground black pepper
8 ounces dried spiral-shaped pasta, such as rotini

Directions

1. **Preparing the Ingredients**. Heat the oil in the Foodi SmartLid turned to the "Sauté" function. Add the onion and cook, often stirring, until softened, about 4 minutes. Add the garlic and cook until aromatic, less than 1 minute.
Crumble in the ground lamb; cook, stirring occasionally until it has lost its raw color, about 5 minutes. Add the eggplant and cook for 1 minute, often stirring, to soften a bit. Pour in the red wine and scrape up any browned bits in the pot as it comes to a simmer.
Stir in the broth, tomato paste, cinnamon, oregano, dill, salt, and pepper until everything is coated in the tomato sauce. Stir in the pasta until coated.
2. **High pressure for 8 minutes**. Lock the pressure cooking lid on the Foodi SmartLid and then cook for 8 minutes. To get 8-minutes cook time, press "Pressure" button and use the Time Adjustment button to adjust the cook time to 8 minutes.
3. **Pressure Release**. Use the quick-release method.
Remove the lid from the Foodi SmartLid. Close air fryer lid. Select BROIL, and set time to 5 minutes. Cooking for an additional 4 minutes if dish needs more browning.
Unlock and open the pot. Stir well before serving.

Beef Stroganoff

PREP: 10 MINUTES • COOK TIME: 14 MINUTES • TOTAL: 24 MINUTES
SERVES: 4

Ingredients
9 Ozs Tender Beef
1 Onion, chopped
1 Tbsp Paprika
3/4 Cup Sour Cream
Salt and Pepper to taste
Baking Dish

Directions:

Preparing the Ingredients. Preheat the Foodi SmartLid to 390 degrees.

Chop the beef and marinate it with the paprika.

Add the chopped onions into the baking dish and heat for about 2 minutes in the Foodi SmartLid.

When the onions are transparent, add the beef into the dish and cook for 5 minutes.

Once the beef is starting to tender, pour in the sour cream and cook for another 7 minutes.

At this point, the liquid should have reduced. Season with salt and pepper and serve.

Lamb Shanks Provençal

PREP: 10 MINUTES • PRESSURE: 40 MINUTES • AIR CRISP: 18 MINUTES • TOTAL: 68 MINUTES
PRESSURE LEVEL: HIGH • RELEASE: NATURAL
SERVES 6

Ingredients
2 large (12-ounce) lamb shanks
1 teaspoon kosher salt, plus additional for seasoning
Freshly ground black pepper
1 tablespoon olive oil
1 cup sliced onion
2 garlic cloves, finely minced
2 medium plum tomatoes, coarsely chopped, or ½ cup diced canned tomatoes, drained
½ cup dry white wine or dry white vermouth
1 cup Chicken Stock or low-sodium broth
1 bay leaf
1 lemon, sliced very thin
⅓ cup pitted Kalamata olives
2 tablespoons coarsely chopped fresh parsley

Directions

1. **Preparing the Ingredients.** Sprinkle the lamb shanks with 1 teaspoon of kosher salt and several grinds of pepper. The longer ahead of the cooking time you can do this, the better. Cover and let sit for 20 minutes to 2 hours at room temperature or refrigerate for up to 24 hours.

   Heat the vegetable oil in the Foodi SmartLid using the "Sauté" function, until the oil is shimmering and flows like water. Add the lamb shanks, and brown on all sides, about 6 minutes total. Remove them to a plate. Add the onion and garlic, and sprinkle with a pinch or two of kosher salt. Cook, stirring, for about 3 minutes, or until the onions just begin to brown. Add the tomatoes, and cook until most of their liquid evaporates.

   Add the white wine, and stir, scraping up the browned bits from the bottom of the cooker.

Cook for 2 to 3 minutes, or until the wine reduces by about half; then add the Chicken Stock and bay leaf. Return the lamb shanks to the cooker, and place the lemon slices over them.

2. **High pressure for 40 minutes**. Lock the pressure cooking lid on the Foodi SmartLid and then cook for 40 minutes. To get 40-minutes cook time, press "Pressure" button and adjust the time.
3. **Pressure Release**. After cooking, use the natural method to release pressure.
4. **Finish the dish**. Remove the lid from the Foodi SmartLid. Close air fryer lid. Select AIR FRY, set temperature to 375°F, and set time to 18 minutes. Check after 10 minutes, cooking for an additional 8 minutes if dish needs more browning.

Transfer the lamb to a cutting board or plate, and tent it with aluminum foil. Strain the sauce into a fat separator, and let it rest until the fat rises to the surface.

If you don't have a fat separator, let the sauce sit for a few minutes, then spoon or blot off any excess fat from the top and discard. Pour the defatted sauce back into the cooker along with the strained vegetables. If you want a thicker sauce, simmer the liquid for about 5 minutes, or until it reaches the desired consistency.

Stir in the olives and parsley. Place the shanks in shallow bowls, pour the sauce and vegetables over the lamb, and serve.

Lamb shanks benefit from salting in advance, which makes them much more flavorful and helps them brown beautifully. If you have the time, salt them up to 24 hours in advance. Place them on a tray and refrigerate, covered loosely with foil.

Beefy Steak Topped with Chimichurri Sauce

PREP: 5 MINUTES • COOK TIME: 60 MINUTES • TOTAL: 65 MINUTES
SERVES: 6

Ingredients
1 cup commercial chimichurri
3 pounds steak
Salt and pepper to taste

Directions:

1. **Preparing the Ingredients.** Place all ingredients in a Ziploc bag and marinate in the fridge for 2 hours.
Preheat the Foodi SmartLid to 390°F.
Place the grill pan accessory in the Foodi SmartLid.
2. **Air Frying**. Close air fryer lid. Grill the skirt steak for 20 minutes per batch.
Flip the steak every 10 minutes for even grilling.

PER SERVING: CALORIES: 507; FAT: 27G; PROTEIN:63 G

Beef Ribeye Steak

PREP: 5 MINUTES • COOK TIME: 20 MINUTES • TOTAL: 25 MINUTES
SERVES: 4

Ingredients
4 (8-ounce) ribeye steaks
1 tablespoon McCormick Grill Mates Montreal Steak Seasoning
Salt
Pepper

Directions:
1. **Preparing the Ingredients.** Season the steaks with the steak seasoning and salt and pepper to taste. Place 2 steaks in the Foodi SmartLid. You can use an accessory grill pan, a layer rack, or the standard Foodi SmartLid basket.
2. **Air Frying.** Close air fryer lid. Cook for 4 minutes. Open the Foodi SmartLid and flip the steaks.
Cook for an additional 4 to 5 minutes. Check for doneness to determine how much additional cook time is need. Remove the cooked steaks from the Foodi SmartLid, then repeat steps 2 through 4 for the remaining 2 steaks. Cool before serving.

PER SERVING: CALORIES: 293; FAT: 22G; PROTEIN:23G; FIBER:0G

Air fryer Roast Beef

PREP: 5 MINUTES • COOK TIME: 45 MINUTES • TOTAL: 50 MINUTES
SERVES: 6

Ingredients
Roast beef
1 tbsp. olive oil
Seasonings of choice

Directions:
1. **Preparing the Ingredients.** Ensure your Foodi SmartLid is preheated to 160 degrees.
Place roast in bowl and toss with olive oil and desired seasonings.
Put seasoned roast into Foodi SmartLid.
2. **Air Frying.** Close air fryer lid. Set temperature to 160°F, and set time to 30 minutes and cook 30 minutes.
Turn roast when the timer sounds and cook another 15 minutes.

PER SERVING: CALORIES: 267; FAT: 8G; PROTEIN:21G; SUGAR:1G

Beef Korma

PREP: 10 MINUTES • COOK TIME: 20 MINUTES • TOTAL: 30 MINUTES
SERVES: 6

Ingredients
½ cup yogurt
1 tablespoon curry powder
1 tablespoon olive oil
1 onion, chopped
2 cloves garlic, minced
1 tomato, diced
½ cup frozen baby peas, thawed

Directions:
1. **Preparing the Ingredients.** In a medium bowl, combine the steak, yogurt, and curry powder. Stir and set aside.
   In a 6-inch metal bowl, combine the olive oil, onion, and garlic.
2. **Air Frying.** Close air fryer lid. Cook for 3 to 4 minutes or until crisp and tender. Add the steak along with the yogurt and the diced tomato. Cook for 12 to 13 minutes or until steak is almost tender. Stir in the peas and cook for 2 to 3 minutes or until hot.

PER SERVING: CALORIES: 289; FAT: 11G; PROTEIN:38G; FIBER:2G

Cumin-Paprika Rubbed Beef Brisket

PREP: 5 MINUTES • COOK TIME: 2 HOURS • TOTAL: 2 HOURS, 5 MINUTES
SERVES: 12

Ingredients
¼ teaspoon cayenne pepper
1 ½ tablespoons paprika
1 teaspoon garlic powder
1 teaspoon ground cumin
1 teaspoon onion powder
2 teaspoons dry mustard
2 teaspoons ground black pepper
2 teaspoons salt
5 pounds brisket roast
5 tablespoons olive oil

Directions:
1. **Preparing the Ingredients.** Place all ingredients in a Ziploc bag and allow to marinate in the fridge for at least 2 hours. Preheat the Foodi SmartLid for 5 minutes. Place the meat in a baking dish that will fit in the Foodi SmartLid.
2. **Air Frying.** Place in the Foodi SmartLid, close air fryer lid and cook for 2 hours at 350°F.

PER SERVING: CALORIES: 269; FAT: 12.8G; PROTEIN:35.6G; FIBER:2G

Lamb Shanks With Pancetta

PREP: 15 MINUTES • PRESSURE: 60 MINUTES • AIR CRISP: 18 MINUTES • TOTAL: 75 MINUTES • PRESSURE LEVEL: HIGH • RELEASE: NATURAL
SERVES 4

Ingredients

2 tablespoons olive oil
One 6-ounce pancetta chunk, chopped
Four 12-ounce lamb shanks
1 small yellow onion, chopped
One 28-ounce can diced tomatoes, drained (about 3½ cups)
1 ounce dried mushrooms, preferably porcini, crumbled
3 tablespoons packed celery leaves, minced
2 tablespoons minced chives
2 cups dry, light white wine, such as Sauvignon Blanc
2 tablespoons all-purpose flour
½ teaspoon ground black pepper

Directions

1. **Preparing the Ingredients**. Heat the oil in the Foodi SmartLid, turned to the "sauté" function. Add the pancetta and brown well, about 6 minutes, stirring often. Use a slotted spoon to transfer the pancetta to a large bowl.

   Add two of the shanks to the cooker; brown on all sides, turning occasionally, about 8 minutes. Transfer them to the bowl and repeat with the remaining shanks.

   Add the onion to the pot; cook, often stirring, until softened, about 4 minutes. Stir in the tomatoes, dried mushroom crumbles, celery leaves, and chives. Cook until bubbling, about minutes, stirring often.

   Whisk the wine, flour, and pepper in a medium bowl until the flour dissolves; stir this mixture into the sauce in the pot. Cook until thickened and bubbling, about 1 minute.

   Return the shanks, pancetta, and their juices to the cooker.

2. **High pressure for 60 minutes.** Close the pressure cooking lid and the pressure valve and then cook for 60 minutes. To get 60-minutes cook time, press "Pressure" button and use the Time Adjustment button to adjust the cook time to 60 minutes.

   Turn off the Foodi SmartLid or unplug it, so it doesn't jump to its keep-warm setting.

3. **Pressure Release**. Let its pressure return to normal naturally, 20 to 30 minutes.

4. **Finish the dish**. Remove the lid from the Foodi SmartLid. Close air fryer lid. Select AIR FRY, set temperature to 375°F, and set time to 18 minutes. Check after 10 minutes, cooking for an additional 8 minutes if dish needs more browning.

   Transfer a shank to each serving bowl. Skim any surface fat from the sauce with a flatware spoon. Ladle the sauce and vegetables over the lamb shanks.

Sugar-And-Spice Beef Empanadas

PREP: 15 MINUTES • COOK TIME: 15 MINUTES • TOTAL: 30 MINUTES
SERVES: 4

Ingredients

6 ounces of raw, lean ground beef
¼ cup of raw white onions, sliced and finely diced
1 teaspoon of cinnamon
½ teaspoon of nutmeg
½ teaspoon of ground cloves
1 small pinch of brown sugar
2 teaspoons of red chilli powder
pre-made empanada dough shells

Directions:

1. **Preparing the Ingredients.** In a deep stovetop saucepan, crumble and cook the ground beef at medium heat. Add in the onions, stirring continuously with a wooden spoon, then add the cinnamon, nutmeg and cloves. Break up the ground beef as it cooks, so it doesn't form large clumps. Remove the saucepan from the stovetop as soon as the beef is fully cooked, the onions are soft, and the spices are releasing their fragrances. Do not overcook, you want the meat to remain moist and juicy. Cover the saucepan and let stand on a heatsafe surface for a few minutes. Lay empanada shells flat on a clean counter. Spoon the spiced cooked beef from the saucepan into the empanada shells – a heaping spoonful on each, though not so much that the mixture spills over the edges. Fold the empanada shells over so that the spiced beef is fully covered. Seal edges with water and press down with a fork to secure. Sprinkle brown sugar over the still-wet seams of the empanadas, for an extra sweet crunch. Cover the basket of the Foodi SmartLid with a lining of tin foil, leaving the edges uncovered to allow air to circulate through the basket.

2. **Air Frying.** Place the empanadas in the foil-lined Foodi SmartLid basket, close air fryer lid and set at 350 degrees for 15 minutes. Halfway through, slide the frying basket out and flip the empanadas using a spatula. Remove when golden, and serve directly from the basket onto plates.

Crispy Mongolian Beef

PREP: 5 MINUTES • COOK TIME: 10 MINUTES • TOTAL: 15 MINUTES
SERVES: 6

Ingredients
Olive oil
½ C. almond flour
2 pounds beef tenderloin or beef chuck, sliced into strips
Sauce:
½ C. chopped green onion
1 tsp. red chili flakes
1 tsp. almond flour
½ C. brown sugar
1 tsp. hoisin sauce
½ C. water
½ C. rice vinegar
½ C. low-sodium soy sauce
1 tbsp. chopped garlic
1 tbsp. finely chopped ginger
2 tbsp. olive oil

Directions:
1. **Preparing the Ingredients.** Toss strips of beef in almond flour, ensuring they are coated well. Add to the Foodi SmartLid.
2. **Air Frying**. Close air fryer lid. Set temperature to 300°F, and set time to 10 minutes, and cook 10 minutes at 300 degrees.
Meanwhile, add all sauce ingredients to the pan and bring to a boil. Mix well. Add beef strips to the sauce and cook 2 minutes.
Serve over cauliflower rice!

PER SERVING: CALORIES: 290; FAT: 14G; PROTEIN:22G; SUGAR:1G

Beef & Lemon Schnitzel for One

PREP: 5 MINUTES • COOK TIME: 12 MINUTES • TOTAL: 17 MINUTES
SERVES: 1

Ingredients
2 Tbsp Oil
2–3 oz Breadcrumbs
1 Whisked Egg in a Saucer/Soup Plate
1 Beef Schnitzel
1 Freshly Picked Lemon

Directions:
1. **Preparing the Ingredients.** Mix the oil and breadcrumbs together until loose and crumbly. Dip the meat into the egg, then into the crumbs. Make sure that it is evenly covered.
2. **Air Frying**. Gently place in the Foodi SmartLid basket, close air fryer lid and cook at 350° F (preheat if needed) until done. The timing will depend on the thickness of the schnitzel, but for a relatively thin one, it should take roughly 12 min. Serve with a lemon half and a garden salad.

Crispy Beef Schnitzel

PREP: 5 MINUTES • **COOK TIME:** 12 MINUTES • **TOTAL:** 17 MINUTES
SERVES: 1

Ingredients
1 beef schnitzel
Salt and ground black pepper, to taste
2 tablespoons olive oil
1/3 cup breadcrumbs
1 egg, whisked

Directions:
Preparing the Ingredients. Season the schnitzel with salt and black pepper.
In a mixing bowl, combine the oil and breadcrumbs. In another shallow bowl, beat the egg until frothy.
Dip the schnitzel in the egg; then, dip it in the oil mixture. Close air fryer lid.
Air-fry at 350 degrees F for 12 minutes.
Enjoy!

Simple Steak

PREP: 6MINUTES • **COOK TIME:** 14 MINUTES • **TOTAL:** 20 MINUTES
SERVES: 2

Ingredients
½ pound quality cuts steak
Salt and freshly ground black pepper, to taste

Directions:
1. **Preparing the Ingredients.** Preheat the Foodi SmartLid to 390 degrees F.
   Rub the steak with salt and pepper evenly.
2. **Air Frying.** Place the steak in the Foodi SmartLid basket, close air fryer lid and cook for about 14 minutes crispy.

Garlic-Cumin And Orange Juice Marinated Steak

PREP: 6 MINUTES • COOK TIME: 60 MINUTES • TOTAL: 66 MINUTES
SERVES: 4

Ingredients
¼ cup orange juice
1 teaspoon ground cumin
2 pounds skirt steak, trimmed from excess fat
2 tablespoons lime juice
2 tablespoons olive oil
4 cloves of garlic, minced
Salt and pepper to taste

Directions:
1 **Preparing the Ingredients.** Place all ingredients in a mixing bowl and allow to marinate in the fridge for at least 2 hours Preheat the Foodi SmartLid to 390°F.
Place the grill pan accessory in the Foodi SmartLid.
2 **Air Frying.** Close air fryer lid. Grill for 15 minutes per batch and flip the beef every 8 minutes for even grilling.
Meanwhile, pour the marinade on a saucepan and allow to simmer for 10 minutes or until the sauce thickens.
Slice the beef and pour over the sauce.

PER SERVING: CALORIES: 568; FAT: 34.7G; PROTEIN:59.1G; SUGAR:1G

Beef Taco Fried Egg Rolls

PREP: 10 MINUTES • COOK TIME: 12 MINUTES • TOTAL: 25 MINUTES
SERVES: 8

Ingredients
1 tsp. cilantro
2 chopped garlic cloves
1 tbsp. olive oil
1 C. shredded Mexican cheese
½ packet taco seasoning
½ can cilantro lime rotel
½ chopped onion
16 egg roll wrappers
1 pound lean ground beef

Directions:
1 **Preparing the Ingredients.** Ensure that your Foodi SmartLid is preheated to 400 degrees.
Add onions and garlic to a skillet, cooking till fragrant. Then add taco seasoning, pepper, salt, and beef, cooking till beef is broke up into tiny pieces and cooked thoroughly.
Add rotel and stir well.
Lay out egg wrappers and brush with water to soften a bit.
Load wrappers with beef filling and add cheese to each.
Fold diagonally to close and use water to secure edges.
Brush filled egg wrappers with olive oil and add to the Foodi SmartLid.
2 **Air Frying.** Close air fryer lid. Set temperature to 400°F, and set time to 8 minutes. Cook 8 minutes, flip, and cook another 4 minutes.
Served sprinkled with cilantro.

PER SERVING: CALORIES: 348; FAT: 11G; PROTEIN:24G; SUGAR:1G

Beef With Beans

PREP: 10 MINUTES • COOK TIME: 13 MINUTES •
TOTAL: 23 MINUTES
SERVES: 8

Ingredients
12 Ozs Lean Steak
1 Onion, sliced
1 Can Chopped Tomatoes
3/4 Cup Beef Stock
4 Tsp Fresh Thyme, chopped
1 Can Red Kidney Beans
Salt and Pepper to taste
Oven Safe Bowl

Directions:
1. **Preparing the Ingredients.** Preheat the Foodi SmartLid to 390 degrees.
   Trim the fat from the meat and cut into thin 1cm strips
   Add onion slices to the oven safe bowl and place in the Foodi SmartLid.
2. **Air Frying**. Close air fryer lid. Cook for 3 minutes. Add the meat and continue cooking for 5 minutes.
   Add the tomatoes and their juice, beef stock, thyme and the beans and cook for an additional 5 minutes
   Season with black pepper to taste.

Swedish Meatballs
PREP: 10 MINUTES • COOK TIME: 14 MINUTES •
TOTAL: 24 MINUTES
SERVES: 4

Ingredients
For the meatballs
1 pound 93% lean ground beef
1 (1-ounce) packet Lipton Onion Recipe Soup & Dip Mix
⅓ cup bread crumbs
1 egg, beaten
Salt
Pepper
For the gravy
1 cup beef broth
⅓ cup heavy cream
3 tablespoons all-purpose flour

Directions:
1. **Preparing the Ingredients.** In a large bowl, combine the ground beef, onion soup mix, bread crumbs, egg, and salt and pepper to taste. Mix thoroughly.
   Using 2 tablespoons of the meat mixture, create each meatball by rolling the beef mixture around in your hands. This should yield about 10 meatballs.
2. **Air Frying**. Place the meatballs in the Foodi SmartLid. It is okay to stack them. Close air fryer lid and cook for 14 minutes.
   While the meatballs cook, prepare the gravy. Heat a saucepan over medium-high heat.
   Add the beef broth and heavy cream. Stir for 1 to 2 minutes.
   Add the flour and stir. Cover and allow the sauce to simmer for 3 to 4 minutes, or until thick.
   Drizzle the gravy over the meatballs and serve.

PER SERVING: CALORIES: 178; FAT: 14G; PROTEIN:9G; FIBER:0G

Rice and Meatball Stuffed Bell Peppers

PREP: 13 MINUTES • COOK TIME: 15 MINUTES • TOTAL: 28 MINUTES
SERVES: 4

Ingredients
4 bell peppers
1 tablespoon olive oil
1 small onion, chopped
2 cloves garlic, minced
1 cup frozen cooked rice, thawed
16 to 20 small frozen precooked meatballs, thawed
½ cup tomato sauce
3 tablespoons Dijon mustard

Directions:
1. **Preparing the Ingredients.** To prepare the peppers, cut off about ½ inch of the tops. Carefully remove the membranes and seeds from inside the peppers. Set aside.
In a 6-by-6-by-2-inch pan, combine the olive oil, onion, and garlic.
2. **Air Frying.** Close air fryer lid. Bake in the Foodi SmartLid for 2 to 4 minutes or until crisp and tender. Remove the vegetable mixture from the pan and set aside in a medium bowl.
Add the rice, meatballs, tomato sauce, and mustard to the vegetable mixture and stir to combine. Stuff the peppers with the meat-vegetable mixture.
Place the peppers in the Foodi SmartLid basket and bake for 9 to 13 minutes or until the filling is hot and the peppers are tender.

PER SERVING: CALORIES: 487; FAT: 21G; PROTEIN:26G; FIBER:6G

Pub Style Corned Beef Egg Rolls

PREP: 15 MINUTES • COOK TIME: 10 MINUTES • TOTAL: 35 MINUTES
SERVES: 10

Ingredients
Olive oil
½ C. orange marmalade
5 slices of Swiss cheese
4 C. corned beef and cabbage
1 egg
10 egg roll wrappers
Brandy Mustard Sauce:
1/16th tsp. pepper
2 tbsp. whole grain mustard
1 tsp. dry mustard powder
1 C. heavy cream
½ C. chicken stock
¼ C. brandy
¾ C. dry white wine
¼ tsp. curry powder
½ tbsp. cilantro
1 minced shallot
2 tbsp. ghee

Directions:
1. **Preparing the Ingredients.** To make mustard sauce, add shallots and ghee to skillet, cooking until softened. Then add brandy and wine, heating to a low boil. Cook 5 minutes for liquids to reduce. Add stock and seasonings. Simmer 5 minutes. Turn down heat and add heavy cream. Cook on low till sauce reduces and it covers the back of a spoon.
Place sauce in the fridge to chill.
Crack the egg in a bowl and set to the side. Lay out an egg wrapper with the corner towards you. Brush the edges with egg wash.
Place 1/3 cup of corned beef mixture into the center along with 2 tablespoons of marmalade and ½ a slice of Swiss cheese.

Fold the bottom corner over filling. As you are folding the sides, make sure they are stick well to the first flap you made. Place filled rolls into prepared Foodi SmartLid basket. Spritz rolls with olive oil.

2. **Air Frying.** Close air fryer lid, set temperature to 390°F, and set time to 10 minutes. Cook 10 minutes at 390 degrees, shaking halfway through cooking.
Serve rolls with Brandy Mustard sauce.

PER SERVING: CALORIES: 415; FAT: 13G; PROTEIN:38G; SUGAR:4G

Stir-Fried Steak and Cabbage

PREP: 15 MINUTES • COOK TIME: 10 MINUTES • TOTAL: 35 MINUTES
SERVES: 4

Ingredients
½ pound sirloin steak, cut into strips
2 teaspoons cornstarch
1 tablespoon peanut oil
2 cups chopped red or green cabbage
1 yellow bell pepper, chopped
2 green onions, chopped
2 cloves garlic, sliced
½ cup commercial stir-fry sauce

Directions:

1. **Preparing the Ingredients.** Toss the steak with the cornstarch and set aside. In a 6-inch metal bowl, combine the peanut oil with the cabbage.
2. **Air Frying.** Place in the basket, close air fryer lid and cook for 3 to 4 minutes. Remove the bowl from the basket and add the steak, pepper, onions, and garlic. Return to the Foodi SmartLid and cook for 3 to 5 minutes or until the steak is cooked to desired doneness and vegetables are crisp and tender.
Add the stir-fry sauce and cook for 2 to 4 minutes or until hot. Serve over rice.

PER SERVING: CALORIES: 180; FAT: 7G; PROTEIN:20G; FIBER:2G

Reuben Egg Rolls

PREP: 5 MINUTES • COOK TIME: 20 MINUTES • TOTAL: 25 MINUTES
SERVES: 6

Ingredients
Swiss cheese
Can of sauerkraut
Sliced deli corned beef
Egg roll wrappers

Directions:
1 **Preparing the Ingredients.** Cut corned beef and Swiss cheese into thin slices. Drain sauerkraut and dry well.
Take egg roll wrapper and moisten edges with water.
Stack center with corned beef and cheese till you reach desired thickness. Top off with sauerkraut.
Fold corner closest to you over the edge of filling. Bring up sides and glue with water.
Add to the Foodi SmartLid basket and spritz with olive oil.
2 **Air Frying.** Close air fryer lid. Set temperature to 400°F, and set time to 4 minutes. Cook 4 minutes at 400 degrees, then flip and cook another 4 minutes.

PER SERVING: CALORIES: 251; FAT: 12G; PROTEIN:31G; SUGAR:4G

Air-Fried Philly Cheesesteak

PREP: 5 MINUTES • COOK TIME: 16 MINUTES • TOTAL: 21 MINUTES
SERVES: 6

Ingredients
Large hoagie bun, sliced in half
6 ounces of sirloin or flank steak, sliced into bite-sized pieces
½ white onion, rinsed and sliced
½ red pepper, rinsed and sliced
slices of American cheese

Directions:
1 **Preparing the Ingredients**. Set the Foodi SmartLid to 320 degrees for 10 minutes.
Arrange the steak pieces, onions and peppers on a piece of tin foil, flat and not overlapping, and set the tin foil on one side of the air-fryer basket. The foil should not take up more than half of the surface; the juices from the steak and the moisture from the vegetables will mingle while cooking.
Lay the hoagie-bun halves, crusty-side up and soft-side down, on the other half of the Foodi SmartLid.
2 **Air Frying**. Close air fryer lid. After 10 minutes, the Foodi SmartLid will shut off; the hoagie buns should be starting to crisp and the steak and vegetables will have begun to cook.
Carefully, flip the hoagie buns so they are now crusty-side down and soft-side up; cover both sides with one slice each of American cheese.
With a long spoon, gently stir the steak, onions and peppers in the foil to ensure even coverage.
Set the Foodi SmartLid to 360 degrees for 6 minutes.
After 6 minutes, when the fryer shuts off, the cheese will be perfectly melted over the toasted bread, and the steak will be

juicy on the inside and crispy on the outside.

Remove the cheesy hoagie halves first, using tongs, and set on a serving plate; then cover one side with the steak, and top with the onions and peppers. Close with the other cheesy hoagie-half, slice into two pieces, and enjoy.

Herbed Roast Beef

PREP: 5 MINUTES • COOK TIME: 20 MINUTES • TOTAL: 25 MINUTES
SERVES: 6

Ingredients
½ tsp. fresh rosemary
1 tsp. dried thyme
¼ tsp. pepper
1 tsp. salt
4-pound top round roast beef
tsp. olive oil

Directions:
1 **Preparing the Ingredients.** Ensure your Foodi SmartLid is preheated to 360 degrees.
   Rub olive oil all over beef.
   Mix rosemary, thyme, pepper, and salt together and proceed to rub all sides of beef with spice mixture.
   Place seasoned beef into Foodi SmartLid.
2 **Air Frying.** Close air fryer lid. Set temperature to 360°F, and set time to 20 minutes.
   Allow roast to rest 10 minutes before slicing to serve.

PER SERVING: CALORIES: 502; FAT: 18G; PROTEIN:48G; SUGAR:2G

Tender Beef with Sour Cream Sauce

PREP: 5 MINUTES • COOK TIME: 12 MINUTES • TOTAL: 17 MINUTES
SERVES: 2

Ingredients
9 ounces tender beef, chopped
1 cup scallions, chopped
2 cloves garlic, smashed
3/4 cup sour cream
3/4 teaspoon salt
1/4 teaspoon black pepper, or to taste
1/2 teaspoon dried dill weed

Directions:
1. **Preparing the Ingredients.** Add the beef, scallions, and garlic to the baking dish.
2. **Air Frying.** Close air fryer lid. Cook for about 5 minutes at 390 degrees F.
   Once the meat is starting to tender, pour in the sour cream. Stir in the salt, black pepper, and dill.
   Now, cook 7 minutes longer.

Beef Empanadas

PREP: 5 MINUTES • COOK TIME: 20 MINUTES • TOTAL: 25 MINUTES
SERVES: 6

Ingredients
1 tsp. water
1 egg white
1 C. picadillo
8 Goya empanada discs (thawed)

Directions:
1. **Preparing the Ingredients.** Ensure your Foodi SmartLid is preheated to 325. Spray basket with olive oil.
   Place 2 tablespoons of picadillo into the center of each disc. Fold disc in half and use a fork to seal edges. Repeat with all ingredients.
   Whisk egg white with water and brush tops of empanadas with egg wash.
   Add 2-3 empanadas to the Foodi SmartLid.
2. **Air Frying.** Close air fryer lid. Set temperature to 325°F, and set time to 8 minutes, cook until golden. Repeat till you cook all filled empanadas.

PER SERVING: CALORIES: 183; FAT: 5G; PROTEIN:11G; SUGAR:2G

Beef Pot Pie

PREP: 5 MINUTES • COOK TIME: 90 MINUTES • TOTAL: 95 MINUTES
SERVES: 2

Ingredients
1 tablespoon olive oil
1 pound beef stewing steak, cubed
1 large onion, chopped
1 tablespoon tomato puree
1 can ale
Warm water, as required
2 beef bouillon cubes
Salt and freshly ground black pepper, to taste
1 tablespoon plain flour plus more for dusting
1 prepared short crust pastry

Directions:
1. **Preparing the Ingredients.** In a pan, heat oil on medium heat. Add steak and cook for about 4-5 minutes. Add onion and cook for about 4-5 minutes.
   Add tomato puree and cook for about 2-3 minutes.
   In a jug, add the ale and enough water to double the mixture.
   Add the ale mixture, cubes, salt and black pepper in the pan with beef and bring to a boil on high heat. Reduce the heat to low and simmer for about 1 hour.
   In a bowl, mix together flour and 3 tablespoons of warm water.
   Slowly, add the flour mixture in beef mixture, stirring continuously.
   Remove from heat and keep aside. Roll out the short crust pastry.
   Line 2 ramekins with pastry and dust with flour.
   Divide the beef mixture in the ramekins evenly.
   Place extra pastry on top.
2. **Air Frying.** Preheat the Foodi SmartLid to 390 degrees F, close air fryer lid and Cook for about 10 minutes.

Now, set the Foodi SmartLid to 335 degrees F, and Cook for about 6 minutes more.

Bolognaise Sauce

PREP: 5 MINUTES • COOK TIME: 30 MINUTES • TOTAL: 35 MINUTES
SERVES: 2

Ingredients
13 Ozs Ground Beef
1 Carrot
1 Stalk of Celery
10 Ozs Diced Tomatoes
1/2 Onion
Salt and Pepper to taste
Oven safe bowl

Directions:
1. **Preparing the Ingredients.** Preheat the Foodi SmartLid to 390 degrees.
   Finely dice the carrot, celery and onions. Place into the oven safe bowl along with the ground beef and combine well
2. **Air Frying.** Place the bowl into the Foodi SmartLid tray, close air fryer lid and cook for 12 minutes until browned.
   Pour the diced tomatoes into the bowl and replace in the Foodi SmartLid.
   Season with salt and pepper, then cook for another 18 minutes
   Serve over cooked pasta or freeze for later use.

Breaded Spam Steaks

PREP: 5 MINUTES • COOK TIME: 5 MINUTES • TOTAL: 10 MINUTES
SERVES: 2

Ingredients
12 Oz Can Luncheon Meat
1 Cup All Purpose Flour
2 Eggs, beaten
2 Cups Italian Seasoned Breadcrumbs

Directions:
1. **Preparing the Ingredients.** Preheat the Foodi SmartLid to 380 degrees.
   Cut the luncheon meat into 1/4 inch slices. Gently press the luncheon meat slices into the flour to coat and shake off the excess flour. Dip into the beaten egg, then press into breadcrumbs.
2. **Air Frying.** Place the battered slices into the Foodi SmartLid tray, close air fryer lid and cook for 3 to 5 minutes until golden brown.
   Serve with chili or tomato sauce

Air Fryer Burgers

PREP: 5 MINUTES • COOK TIME: 10 MINUTES • TOTAL: 15 MINUTES
SERVES: 4

Ingredients
1 pound lean ground beef
1 tsp. dried parsley
½ tsp. dried oregano
½ tsp. pepper
½ tsp. salt
½ tsp. onion powder
½ tsp. garlic powder
Few drops of liquid smoke
1 tsp. Worcestershire sauce

Directions:
1. **Preparing the Ingredients.** Ensure your Foodi SmartLid is preheated to 350 degrees.
   Mix all seasonings together till combined. Place beef in a bowl and add seasonings. Mix well, but do not overmix.
   Make 4 patties from the mixture and using your thumb, making an indent in the center of each patty.
   Add patties to Foodi SmartLid basket.
2. **Air Frying.** Close air fryer lid. Set temperature to 350°F, and set time to 10 minutes, and cook 10 minutes. No need to turn.

PER SERVING: CALORIES: 148; FAT: 5G; PROTEIN:24G; SUGAR:1G

Cheese-Stuffed Meatballs

PREP: 10 MINUTES • COOK TIME: 10 MINUTES • TOTAL: 20 MINUTES
SERVES: 4

Ingredients
⅓ cup soft bread crumbs
3 tablespoons milk
1 tablespoon ketchup
1 egg
½ teaspoon dried marjoram
Pinch salt
Freshly ground black pepper
1 pound 95 percent lean ground beef
20 ½-inch cubes of cheese
Olive oil for misting

Directions:
1. **Preparing the Ingredients.** In a large bowl, combine the bread crumbs, milk, ketchup, egg, marjoram, salt, and pepper, and mix well. Add the ground beef and mix gently but thoroughly with your hands. Form the mixture into 20 meatballs. Shape each meatball around a cheese cube. Mist the meatballs with olive oil and put into the Foodi SmartLid basket.
2. **Air Frying.** Close air fryer lid. Bake for 10 to 13 minutes or until the meatballs register 165°F on a meat thermometer.

PER SERVING: CALORIES: 393; FAT: 17G; PROTEIN:50G; FIBER:0G

Roasted Stuffed Peppers

PREP: 5 MINUTES • COOK TIME: 20 MINUTES • TOTAL: 25 MINUTES
SERVES: 4

Ingredients
4 ounces shredded cheddar cheese
½ tsp. pepper
½ tsp. salt
1 tsp. Worcestershire sauce
½ C. tomato sauce
8 ounces lean ground beef
1 tsp. olive oil
1 minced garlic clove
½ chopped onion
2 green peppers

Directions:
1. **Preparing the Ingredients.** Ensure your Foodi SmartLid is preheated to 390 degrees. Spray with olive oil.
   Cut stems off bell peppers and remove seeds. Cook in boiling salted water for 3 minutes.
   Sauté garlic and onion together in a skillet until golden in color.
   Take skillet off the heat. Mix pepper, salt, Worcestershire sauce, ¼ cup of tomato sauce, half of cheese and beef together.
   Divide meat mixture into pepper halves.
   Top filled peppers with remaining cheese and tomato sauce.
   Place filled peppers in the Foodi SmartLid.
2. **Air Frying.** Close air fryer lid. Set temperature to 390°F, and set time to 20 minutes, bake 15-20 minutes.

PER SERVING: CALORIES: 295; FAT: 8G; PROTEIN:23G; SUGAR:2G

Air Fried Steak Sandwich

PREP: 5 MINUTES • COOK TIME: 16 MINUTES • TOTAL: 21 MINUTES
SERVES: 4

Ingredients
Large hoagie bun, sliced in half
6 ounces of sirloin or flank steak, sliced into bite-sized pieces
½ tablespoon of mustard powder
½ tablespoon of soy sauce
1 tablespoon of fresh bleu cheese, crumbled
8 medium-sized cherry tomatoes, sliced in half
1 cup of fresh arugula, rinsed and patted dry

Directions:
1. **Preparing the Ingredients.** In a small mixing bowl, combine the soy sauce and onion powder; stir with a fork until thoroughly combined.
   Lay the raw steak strips in the soy-mustard mixture, and fully immerse each piece to marinate.
   Set the Foodi SmartLid to 320 degrees for 10 minutes.
   Arrange the soy-mustard marinated steak pieces on a piece of tin foil, flat and not overlapping, and set the tin foil on one side of the Foodi SmartLid basket. The foil should not take up more than half of the surface.
   Lay the hoagie-bun halves, crusty-side up and soft-side down, on the other half of the air-fryer.
2. **Air Frying.** Close air fryer lid.
   After 10 minutes, the Foodi SmartLid will shut off; the hoagie buns should be starting to crisp and the steak will have begun to cook.
   Carefully, flip the hoagie buns so they are now crusty-side down and soft-side up; crumble a layer of the bleu cheese on each hoagie half.

With a long spoon, gently stir the marinated steak in the foil to ensure even coverage.

Set the Foodi SmartLid to 360 degrees for 6 minutes.

After 6 minutes, when the fryer shuts off, the bleu cheese will be perfectly melted over the toasted bread, and the steak will be juicy on the inside and crispy on the outside.

Remove the cheesy hoagie halves first, using tongs, and set on a serving plate; then cover one side with the steak, and top with the cherry-tomato halves and the arugula. Close with the other cheesy hoagie-half, slice into two pieces, and enjoy.

Carrot and Beef Cocktail Balls

PREP: 5 MINUTES • COOK TIME: 20 MINUTES • TOTAL: 25 MINUTES
SERVES: 10

Ingredients
1 pound ground beef
2 carrots
1 red onion, peeled and chopped
2 cloves garlic
1/2 teaspoon dried rosemary, crushed
1/2 teaspoon dried basil
1 teaspoon dried oregano
1 egg
3/4 cup breadcrumbs
1/2 teaspoon salt
1/2 teaspoon black pepper, or to taste
1 cup plain flour

Directions:
1. **Preparing the Ingredients.** Place ground beef in a large bowl. In a food processor, pulse the carrot, onion and garlic; transfer the vegetable mixture to a large-sized bowl.
   Then, add the rosemary, basil, oregano, egg, breadcrumbs, salt, and black pepper.
   Shape the mixture into even balls; refrigerate for about 30 minutes. Roll the balls into the flour.
2. **Air Frying.** Close air fryer lid. Then, air-fry the balls at 350 degrees F for about 20 minutes, turning occasionally; work with batches. Serve with toothpicks.

Beef Steaks with Beans

PREP: 5 MINUTES • COOK TIME: 10 MINUTES • TOTAL: 15 MINUTES
SERVES: 4

Ingredients
4 beef steaks, trim the fat and cut into strips
1 cup green onions, chopped
2 cloves garlic, minced
1 red bell pepper, seeded and thinly sliced
1 can tomatoes, crushed
1 can cannellini beans
3/4 cup beef broth
1/4 teaspoon dried basil
1/2 teaspoon cayenne pepper
1/2 teaspoon sea salt
1/4 teaspoon ground black pepper, or to taste

Directions:
1. **Preparing the Ingredients**. Add the steaks, green onions and garlic to the Foodi SmartLid basket.
2. **Air Frying**. Close air fryer lid. Cook at 390 degrees F for 10 minutes, working in batches.
Stir in the remaining ingredients and cook for an additional 5 minutes.

Air Fryer Beef Steak

PREP: 5 MINUTES • COOK TIME: 15 MINUTES • TOTAL: 20 MINUTES
SERVES: 4

Ingredients
1 tbsp. olive oil
Pepper and salt
2 pounds of ribeye steak

Directions:
1. **Preparing the Ingredients.** Season meat on both sides with pepper and salt. Rub all sides of meat with olive oil. Preheat Foodi SmartLid to 356 degrees and spritz with olive oil.
2. **Air Frying**. Close air fryer lid. Set temperature to 356°F, and set time to 7 minutes. Cook steak 7 minutes. Flip and cook an additional 6 minutes.
Let meat sit 2-5 minutes to rest. Slice and serve with salad.

PER SERVING: CALORIES: 233; FAT: 19G; PROTEIN:16G; SUGAR:0G

Mushroom Meatloaf

PREP: 5 MINUTES • COOK TIME: 25 MINUTES • TOTAL: 30 MINUTES
SERVES: 4

Ingredients
14-ounce lean ground beef
1 chorizo sausage, chopped finely
1 small onion, chopped
1 garlic clove, minced
2 tablespoons fresh cilantro, chopped
3 tablespoons breadcrumbs
1 egg
Salt and freshly ground black pepper, to taste
2 tablespoons fresh mushrooms, sliced thinly
3 tablespoons olive oil

Directions:
1. **Preparing the Ingredients.** Preheat the Foodi SmartLid to 390 degrees F.
   In a large bowl, add all ingredients except mushrooms and mix till well combined.
   In a baking pan, place the beef mixture.
   With the back of spatula, smooth the surface.
   Top with mushroom slices and gently, press into the meatloaf.
   Drizzle with oil evenly.
2. **Air Frying.** Arrange the pan in the Foodi SmartLid basket, close air fryer lid and cook for about 25 minutes.
   Cut the meatloaf in desires size wedges and serve.

Beef and Broccoli

PREP: 10 MINUTES • COOK TIME: 12 MINUTES • TOTAL: 25 MINUTES
SERVES: 4

Ingredients
1 minced garlic clove
1 sliced ginger root
1 tbsp. olive oil
1 tsp. almond flour
1 tsp. sweetener of choice
1 tsp. low-sodium soy sauce
1/3 C. sherry
2 tsp. sesame oil
1/3 C. oyster sauce
1 pounds of broccoli
¾ pound round steak

Directions:
1. **Preparing the Ingredients.** Remove stems from broccoli and slice into florets. Slice steak into thin strips.
   Combine sweetener, soy sauce, sherry, almond flour, sesame oil, and oyster sauce together, stirring till sweetener dissolves. Put strips of steak into the mixture and allow to marinate 45 minutes to 2 hours. Add broccoli and marinated steak to Foodi SmartLid. Place garlic, ginger, and olive oil on top.
2. **Air Frying.** Close air fryer lid. Set temperature to 400°F, and set time to 12 minutes. Cook 12 minutes at 400 degrees. Serve with cauliflower rice!

PER SERVING: CALORIES: 384; FAT: 16G; PROTEIN:19G; SUGAR:4G

Air Fryer Beef Fajitas

PREP: 5 MINUTES • COOK TIME: 20 MINUTES • TOTAL: 25 MINUTES
SERVES: 6

Ingredients
Beef:
1/8 C. carne asada seasoning
2 pounds beef flap meat
Diet 7-Up
Fajita veggies:
1 tsp. chili powder
1-2 tsp. pepper
1-2 tsp. salt
2 bell peppers, your choice of color
1 onion

Directions:

1. **Preparing the Ingredients.** Slice flap meat into manageable pieces and place into a bowl. Season meat with carne seasoning and pour diet soda over meat. Cover and chill overnight.
Ensure your Foodi SmartLid is preheated to 380 degrees.
Place a parchment liner into the Foodi SmartLid basket and spray with olive oil. Place beef in layers into the basket.
Cook 8-10 minutes, making sure to flip halfway through. Remove and set to the side.
Slice up veggies and spray Foodi SmartLid basket. Add veggies to the fryer and spray with olive oil.

2. **Air Frying.** Close air fryer lid. Set temperature to 400°F, and set time to 10 minutes. Cook 10 minutes at 400 degrees, shaking 1-2 times during cooking process. Serve meat and veggies on wheat tortillas and top with favorite keto fillings!

PER SERVING: CALORIES: 412; FAT: 21G; PROTEIN:13G; SUGAR:1G

Seafood Recipes

Coconut Shrimp

PREP: 5 MINUTES • COOK TIME: 10 MINUTES • TOTAL: 15 MINUTES
SERVES: 3

Ingredients
1 C. almond flour
1 C. panko breadcrumbs
1 tbsp. coconut flour
1 C. unsweetened, dried coconut
1 egg white
12 raw large shrimp

Directions:
1. **Preparing the Ingredients.** Put shrimp on paper towels to drain.
   Mix coconut and panko breadcrumbs together. Then mix in coconut flour and almond flour in a different bowl. Set to the side.
   Dip shrimp into flour mixture, then into egg white, and then into coconut mixture. Place into Foodi SmartLid basket. Repeat with remaining shrimp.
2. **Air Frying**. Close air fryer lid. Set temperature to 350°F, and set time to 10 minutes. Turn halfway through cooking process.

PER SERVING: CALORIES:213; FAT: 8G; PROTEIN:15G; SUGAR:3G

Bacon Wrapped Shrimp

PREP: 5 MINUTES • COOK TIME: 5 MINUTES • TOTAL: 10 MINUTES
SERVES: 4

Ingredients
1¼ pound tiger shrimp, peeled and deveined
1 pound bacon

Directions:
1. **Preparing the Ingredients.** Wrap each shrimp with a slice of bacon.
   Refrigerate for about 20 minutes.
   Preheat the Foodi SmartLid to 390 degrees F.
2. **Air Frying.** Arrange the shrimp in the Foodi SmartLid basket. Close air fryer lid, cook for about 5-7 minutes.

Shrimp And Tomatillo Casserole

PREP: 10 MINUTES • PRESSURE: 9 MINUTES • BROIL: 5 MINUTES • TOTAL: 30 MINUTES • PRESSURE LEVEL: HIGH • RELEASE: QUICK
SERVES 4

Ingredients

2 tablespoons olive oil
1 medium yellow onion, chopped
1 small fresh jalapeño chile, stemmed, seeded, and minced
2 teaspoons minced garlic
1½ pounds fresh tomatillos, husked and chopped
½ cup bottled clam juice
2 tablespoons fresh lime juice
1½ pounds medium shrimp (about 30 per pound), peeled and deveined
¼ cup loosely packed fresh cilantro leaves, chopped
1 cup shredded Monterey jack cheese (about 4 ounces)

Directions

1. **Preparing the Ingredients.** Heat the oil in the Foodi SmartLid turned to the "Browning" function. Add the onion and cook, often stirring, until translucent, about 3 minutes.
   Add the jalapeño and garlic; cook until aromatic, stirring all the while, less than a minute.
   Stir in the tomatillos, clam juice, and lime juice.
2. **High pressure for 9 minutes.** Lock the pressure cooking lid on the Foodi SmartLid and then cook for 9 minutes. To get 9-minutes cook time, press "Pressure" button and use the Time Adjustment button to adjust the cook time to 9 minutes.
3. **Pressure Release** Use the quick-release method.
4. **Finish the dish.** Unlock and open the pot. Turn the Foodi SmartLid to its "Sauté" function. Stir in the shrimp and cilantro; cook for 2 minutes, stirring frequently. Sprinkle the cheese over the top of the casserole. Close air fryer lid and select Broil, set time to 5 minutes. Press Start button to begin.
Serve and enjoy.

Grilled Salmon

PREP: 5 MINUTES • COOK TIME: 10 MINUTES •
TOTAL: 15 MINUTES
SERVES: 3

Ingredients
2 Salmon Fillets
1/2 Tsp Lemon Pepper
1/2 Tsp Garlic Powder
Salt and Pepper
1/3 Cup Soy Sauce
1/3 Cup Sugar
1 Tbsp Olive Oil

Directions:
1. **Preparing the Ingredients.** Season salmon fillets with lemon pepper, garlic powder and salt. In a shallow bowl, add a third cup of water and combine the olive oil, soy sauce and sugar. Place salmon the bowl and immerse in the sauce. Cover with cling film and allow to marinate in the refrigerator for at least an hour
2. **Air Frying.** Preheat the Foodi SmartLid at 350 degrees.
   Place salmon into the Foodi SmartLid, close air fryer lid and cook for 10 minutes or more until the fish is tender.
   Serve with lemon wedges

Air Fryer Salmon

PREP: 5 MINUTES • COOK TIME: 10 MINUTES •
TOTAL: 15 MINUTES
SERVES: 2

Ingredients
½ tsp. salt
½ tsp. garlic powder
½ tsp. smoked paprika
Salmon

Directions:
1. **Preparing the Ingredients.** Mix spices together and sprinkle onto salmon. Place seasoned salmon into the Foodi SmartLid -Pot.
2. **Air Frying.** Close air fryer lid. Set temperature to 400°F, and set time to 10 minutes.

PER SERVING: CALORIES: 185; FAT: 11G; PROTEIN:21G; SUGAR:0G

Beer Potato Fish

PREP: 15 MINUTES • PRESSURE: 40 MINUTES • BROIL: 5 MINUTES • TOTAL: 60 MINUTES • PRESSURE LEVEL: LOW • RELEASE: NATURAL
SERVES 6

Ingredients
1 pound fish fillet
4 medium size potatoes, peeled and diced
1 cup beer
1 red pepper sliced
1 tablespoon oil
1 tablespoon oyster flavored sauce
1 tablespoon rock candy
1 teaspoon salt

Directions
1. **Preparing the Ingredients**. Put all ingredients into your Foodi SmartLid.
2. **High pressure for 40 minutes**. Lock the pressure cooking lid on the Foodi SmartLid and then cook for 40 minutes. To get 40-minutes cook time, press "Pressure" button and use the Time Adjustment button to adjust the cook time to 40 minutes.
3. **Pressure Release**. Release the pressure using natural release method.
4. **Finish the dish**. Close the air fryer lid. Select BROIL, and set the time to 5 minutes. Select START to begin. Cook until top is browned.
Then that is it! Simple, fast, delicious, retaining flavour and nutrition, consistent results all the time.
Serve and Enjoy!

Per Serving Calories: 250.3; Fat: 4.8g; Sodium: 1146.8mg; Fiber: 2.5g; Protien: 25.6g

Steamed Salmon & Sauce

PREP: 5 MINUTES • COOK TIME: 10 MINUTES • TOTAL: 15 MINUTES
SERVES: 2

Ingredients
1 cup Water
2 x 6 oz Fresh Salmon
2 Tsp Vegetable Oil
A Pinch of Salt for Each Fish
½ cup Plain Greek Yogurt
½ cup Sour Cream
2 Tbsp Finely Chopped Dill (Keep a bit for garnishing)
A Pinch of Salt to Taste

Directions:
1. **Preparing the Ingredients.** Pour the water into the bottom of the fryer and start heating to 285° F.
Drizzle oil over the fish and spread it. Salt the fish to taste.
2. **Air Frying**. Close air fryer lid, now pop it into the fryer for 10 min.
In the meantime, mix the yogurt, cream, dill and a bit of salt to make the sauce. When the fish is done, serve with the sauce and garnish with sprigs of dill.

Sweet And Savory Breaded Shrimp

PREP: 5 MINUTES • COOK TIME: 20 MINUTES • TOTAL: 25 MINUTES
SERVES: 2

Ingredients
½ pound of fresh shrimp, peeled from their shells and rinsed
2 raw eggs
½ cup of breadcrumbs (we like Panko, but any brand or home recipe will do)
½ white onion, peeled and rinsed and finely chopped
1 teaspoon of ginger-garlic paste
½ teaspoon of turmeric powder
½ teaspoon of red chili powder
½ teaspoon of cumin powder
½ teaspoon of black pepper powder
½ teaspoon of dry mango powder
Pinch of salt

Directions:
1. **Preparing the Ingredients.** Cover the basket of the Foodi SmartLid with a lining of tin foil, leaving the edges uncovered to allow air to circulate through the basket.
Preheat the Foodi SmartLid to 350 degrees.
In a large mixing bowl, beat the eggs until fluffy and until the yolks and whites are fully combined.
Dunk all the shrimp in the egg mixture, fully submerging.
In a separate mixing bowl, combine the bread crumbs with all the dry ingredients until evenly blended.
One by one, coat the egg-covered shrimp in the mixed dry ingredients so that fully covered, and place on the foil-lined air-fryer basket.
2. **Air Frying**. Close air fryer lid. Set the air-fryer timer to 20 minutes.
Halfway through the cooking time, shake the handle of the air-fryer so that the breaded shrimp jostles inside and fry-coverage is even.
After 20 minutes, when the fryer shuts off, the shrimp will be perfectly cooked and their breaded crust golden-brown and delicious! Using tongs, remove from the Foodi SmartLid and set on a serving dish to cool.

Indian Fish Fingers

PREP: 35 MINUTES • COOK TIME: 15 MINUTES • TOTAL: 50 MINUTES
SERVES: 4

Ingredients
1/2 pound fish fillet
1 tablespoon finely chopped fresh mint leaves or any fresh herbs
1/3 cup bread crumbs
1 teaspoon ginger garlic paste or ginger and garlic powders
1 hot green chili finely chopped
1/2 teaspoon paprika
Generous pinch of black pepper
Salt to taste
3/4 tablespoons lemon juice
3/4 teaspoons garam masala powder
1/3 teaspoon rosemary
1 egg

Directions:
1. **Preparing the Ingredients.** Start by removing any skin on the fish, washing, and patting dry. Cut the fish into fingers.
   In a medium bowl mix together all ingredients except for fish, mint, and bread crumbs. Bury the fingers in the mixture and refrigerate for 30 minutes.
   Remove from the bowl from the fridge and mix in mint leaves.
   In a separate bowl beat the egg, pour bread crumbs into a third bowl. Dip the fingers in the egg bowl then toss them in the bread crumbs bowl.
2. **Air Frying.** Close air fryer lid. Cook at 360 degrees for 15 minutes, toss the fingers halfway through.

PER SERVING: CALORIES: 187; FAT: 7G; PROTEIN:11G; FIBER:1G

Healthy Fish and Chips

PREP: 5 MINUTES • COOK TIME: 15 MINUTES • TOTAL: 20 MINUTES
SERVES: 3

Ingredients
Old Bay seasoning
½ C. panko breadcrumbs
1 egg
2 tbsp. almond flour
4-6 ounce tilapia fillets
Frozen crinkle cut fries

Directions:
1. **Preparing the Ingredients.** Add almond flour to one bowl, beat egg in another bowl, and add panko breadcrumbs to the third bowl, mixed with Old Bay seasoning. Dredge tilapia in flour, then egg, and then breadcrumbs.
   Place coated fish in Foodi SmartLid along with fries.
2. **Air Frying.** Close air fryer lid. Set temperature to 390°F, and set time to 15 minutes.

PER SERVING: CALORIES: 219; FAT: 5G; PROTEIN:25G; SUGAR:1G

Quick Paella

PREP: 7 MINUTES • COOK TIME: 15 MINUTES • TOTAL: 22 MINUTES
SERVES: 4

Ingredients
1 (10-ounce) package frozen cooked rice, thawed
1 (6-ounce) jar artichoke hearts, drained and chopped
¼ cup vegetable broth
½ teaspoon turmeric
½ teaspoon dried thyme
1 cup frozen cooked small shrimp
½ cup frozen baby peas
1 tomato, diced

Directions:

1. **Preparing the Ingredients.** In a 6-by-6-by-2-inch pan, combine the rice, artichoke hearts, vegetable broth, turmeric, and thyme, and stir gently.

2. **Air Frying.** Place in the Foodi SmartLid, close air fryer lid and bake for 8 to 9 minutes or until the rice is hot. Remove from the Foodi SmartLid and gently stir in the shrimp, peas, and tomato. Cook for 5 to 8 minutes or until the shrimp and peas are hot and the paella is bubbling.

PER SERVING: CALORIES: 345; FAT: 1G; PROTEIN:18G; FIBER:4G

Coconut Shrimp

PREP: 15 MINUTES • COOK TIME: 5 MINUTES • TOTAL: 20 MINUTES
SERVES: 4

Ingredients
1 (8-ounce) can crushed pineapple
½ cup sour cream
¼ cup pineapple preserves
2 egg whites
⅔ cup cornstarch
⅔ cup sweetened coconut
1 cup panko bread crumbs
1 pound uncooked large shrimp, thawed if frozen, deveined and shelled
Olive oil for misting

Directions:

1. **Preparing the Ingredients.** Drain the crushed pineapple well, reserving the juice. In a small bowl, combine the pineapple, sour cream, and preserves, and mix well. Set aside. In a shallow bowl, beat the egg whites with 2 tablespoons of the reserved pineapple liquid. Place the cornstarch on a plate. Combine the coconut and bread crumbs on another plate. Dip the shrimp into the cornstarch, shake it off, then dip into the egg white mixture and finally into the coconut mixture. Place the shrimp in the Foodi SmartLid basket and mist with oil.

2. **Air Frying.** Close air fryer lid. Air-fry for 5 to 7 minutes or until the shrimp are crisp and golden brown

PER SERVING: CALORIES: 524; FAT: 14G; PROTEIN:33G; FIBER:4G

3-Ingredient Air Fryer Catfish

PREP: 5 MINUTES • COOK TIME: 13 MINUTES • TOTAL: 20 MINUTES
SERVES: 4

Ingredients
1 tbsp. chopped parsley
1 tbsp. olive oil
¼ C. seasoned fish fry
4 catfish fillets

Directions:
1. **Preparing the Ingredients.** Ensure your Foodi SmartLid is preheated to 400 degrees.
   Rinse off catfish fillets and pat dry.
   Add fish fry seasoning to Ziploc baggie, then catfish. Shake bag and ensure fish gets well coated.
   Spray each fillet with olive oil.
   Add fillets to Foodi SmartLid basket.
2. **Air Frying.** Close air fryer lid. Set temperature to 400°F, and set time to 10 minutes.
   Cook 10 minutes. Then flip and cook another 2-3 minutes.

PER SERVING: CALORIES: 208; FAT: 5G; PROTEIN:17G; SUGAR:0.5G

Tuna Veggie Stir-Fry

PREP: 5 MINUTES • COOK TIME: 12 MINUTES • TOTAL: 17 MINUTES
SERVES: 4

Ingredients
1 tablespoon olive oil
1 red bell pepper, chopped
1 cup green beans, cut into 2-inch pieces
1 onion, sliced
2 cloves garlic, sliced
2 tablespoons low-sodium soy sauce
1 tablespoon honey
½ pound fresh tuna, cubed

Directions:
1. **Preparing the Ingredients.** In a 6-inch metal bowl, combine the olive oil, pepper, green beans, onion, and garlic.
2. **Air Frying.** Close air fryer lid. Cook in the Foodi SmartLid for 4 to 6 minutes, stirring once, until crisp and tender. Add soy sauce, honey, and tuna, and stir. Cook for another 3 to 6 minutes, stirring once, until the tuna is cooked as desired. Tuna can be served rare or medium-rare, or you can cook it until well done.

PER SERVING: CALORIES: 187; FAT: 8G; PROTEIN:17G; FIBER:2G

Salmon Quiche

PREP: 5 MINUTES • COOK TIME: 12 MINUTES • TOTAL: 17 MINUTES
SERVES: 4

Ingredients
5 Ozs Salmon Fillet
1/2 Tbsp Lemon Juice
1/2 Cup Flour
1/4 Cup Butter, melted
2 Eggs and 1 Egg Yolk
3 Tbsps Whipped Cream
Tsps Mustard
Black Pepper to taste
Salt and Pepper
* Quiche Pan

Directions:
1. **Preparing the Ingredients.** Clean and cut the salmon into small cubes.
   Heat the Foodi SmartLid to 375 degrees
   Pour the lemon juice over the salmon cubes and allow to marinate for an hour.
   Combine a tablespoon of water with the butter, flour and yolk in a large bowl. Using your hands, knead the mixture until smooth
   On a clean surface, use a rolling pin to form a circle of dough. Place this into the quiche pan, using your fingers to adhere the pastry to the edges
   Whisk the cream, mustard and eggs together. Season with salt and pepper. Add the marinated salmon into the bowl and combine.
   Pour the content of the bowl into the dough lined quiche pan
2. **Air Frying.** Put the pan in the Foodi SmartLid tray, close air fryer lid and cook for 25 minutes until browned and crispy.

Cilantro-Lime Fried Shrimp

PREP: 10 MINUTES • COOK TIME: 10 MINUTES • TOTAL: 20 MINUTES
SERVES: 4

Ingredients
1 pound raw shrimp, peeled and deveined with tails on or off (see Prep tip)
½ cup chopped fresh cilantro
Juice of 1 lime
1 egg
½ cup all-purpose flour
¾ cup bread crumbs
Salt
Pepper
Cooking oil
½ cup cocktail sauce (optional)

Directions:
1. **Preparing the Ingredients.** Place the shrimp in a plastic bag and add the cilantro and lime juice. Seal the bag. Shake to combine. Marinate in the refrigerator for 30 minutes.
   In a small bowl, beat the egg. In another small bowl, place the flour. Place the bread crumbs in a third small bowl, and season with salt and pepper to taste.
   Spray the Foodi SmartLid basket with cooking oil.
   Remove the shrimp from the plastic bag. Dip each in the flour, then the egg, and then the bread crumbs.
2. **Air Frying.** Place the shrimp in the Foodi SmartLid. It is okay to stack them. Spray the shrimp with cooking oil. Close air fryer lid and cook for 4 minutes.
   Open the Foodi SmartLid and flip the shrimp. I recommend flipping individually instead of shaking to keep the breading intact. Cook for an additional 4 minutes, or until crisp.
   Cool before serving. Serve with cocktail sauce if desired.

PER SERVING: CALORIES: 254; FAT:4G; PROTEIN:29G; FIBER:1G

Lemony Tuna

PREP: 10 MINUTES • COOK TIME: 10 MINUTES • TOTAL: 20 MINUTES
SERVES: 4

Ingredients
2 (6-ounce) cans water packed plain tuna
2 teaspoons Dijon mustard
½ cup breadcrumbs
1 tablespoon fresh lime juice
2 tablespoons fresh parsley, chopped
1 egg
Foodi SmartLid of hot sauce
3 tablespoons canola oil
Salt and freshly ground black pepper, to taste

Directions:
1. **Preparing the Ingredients.** Drain most of the liquid from the canned tuna.
   In a bowl, add the fish, mustard, crumbs, citrus juice, parsley and hot sauce and mix till well combined. Add a little canola oil if it seems too dry. Add egg, salt and stir to combine. Make the patties from tuna mixture. Refrigerate the tuna patties for about 2 hours.
2. **Air Frying.** Preheat the Foodi SmartLid to 355 degrees F. Close air fryer lid and cook for about 10-12 minutes

Bang Bang Panko Breaded Fried Shrimp

PREP: 5 MINUTES • COOK TIME: 8 MINUTES • TOTAL: 13 MINUTES
SERVES: 4

Ingredients
1 tsp. paprika
Montreal chicken seasoning
¾ C. panko bread crumbs
½ C. almond flour
1 egg white
1 pound raw shrimp (peeled and deveined)

Bang Bang Sauce:
¼ C. sweet chili sauce
2 tbsp. sriracha sauce
1/3 C. plain Greek yogurt

Directions:
1. **Preparing the Ingredients.** Ensure your Foodi SmartLid is preheated to 400 degrees.
   Season all shrimp with seasonings.
   Add flour to one bowl, egg white in another, and breadcrumbs to a third.
   Dip seasoned shrimp in flour, then egg whites, and then breadcrumbs.
   Spray coated shrimp with olive oil and add to Foodi SmartLid basket.
2. **Air Frying**. Close air fryer lid. Set temperature to 400°F, and set time to 4 minutes. Cook 4 minutes, flip, and cook an additional 4 minutes.
   To make the sauce, mix together all sauce ingredients until smooth.

PER SERVING: CALORIES: 212; CARBS:12; FAT: 1G; PROTEIN:37G; SUGAR:0.5G

Grilled Soy Salmon Fillets

PREP: 5 MINUTES • COOK TIME: 8 MINUTES • TOTAL: 13 MINUTES
SERVES: 4

Ingredients
4 salmon fillets
1/4 teaspoon ground black pepper
1/2 teaspoon cayenne pepper
1/2 teaspoon salt
1 teaspoon onion powder
1 tablespoon fresh lemon juice
1/2 cup soy sauce
1/2 cup water
1 tablespoon honey
2 tablespoons extra-virgin olive oil

Directions:
1. **Preparing the Ingredients.** Firstly, pat the salmon fillets dry using kitchen towels. Season the salmon with black pepper, cayenne pepper, salt, and onion powder.
   To make the marinade, combine together the lemon juice, soy sauce, water, honey, and olive oil. Marinate the salmon for at least 2 hours in your refrigerator.
   Arrange the fish fillets on a grill basket in your Foodi SmartLid.
2. **Air Frying**. Close air fryer lid and bake at 330 degrees for 8 to 9 minutes, or until salmon fillets are easily flaked with a fork. Work with batches and serve warm.

Flying Fish

PREP: 5 MINUTES • COOK TIME: 12 MINUTES • TOTAL: 17 MINUTES
SERVES: 6

Ingredients
4 Tbsp Oil
3–4 oz Breadcrumbs
1 Whisked Whole Egg in a Saucer/Soup Plate
4 Fresh Fish Fillets
Fresh Lemon (For serving)

Directions:
1. **Preparing the Ingredients.** Preheat the Foodi SmartLid (if necessary) to 350° F. Mix the crumbs and oil until it looks nice and loose.
   Dip the fish in the egg and coat lightly, then move on to the crumbs. Make sure the fillet is covered evenly.
2. **Air Frying.** Close air fryer lid. Cook in the Foodi SmartLid basket for roughly 12 minutes – depending on the size of the fillets you are using.
   Serve with fresh lemon & chips to complete the duo.

Pistachio-Crusted Lemon-Garlic Salmon

PREP: 5 MINUTES • COOK TIME: 20 MINUTES • TOTAL: 25 MINUTES
SERVES: 6

Ingredients
4 medium-sized salmon filets
2 raw eggs
3 ounces of melted butter
1 clove of garlic, peeled and finely minced
1 large-sized lemon
1 teaspoon of salt
1 tablespoon of parsley, rinsed, patted dry and chopped
1 teaspoon of dill, rinsed, patted dry and chopped
½ cup of pistachio nuts, shelled and coarsely crushed

Directions:
1. **Preparing the Ingredients.** Cover the basket of the Foodi SmartLid with a lining of tin foil, leaving the edges uncovered to allow air to circulate through the basket.
   Preheat the Foodi SmartLid to 350 degrees.
   In a mixing bowl, beat the eggs until fluffy and until the yolks and whites are fully combined.
   Add the melted butter, the juice of the lemon, the minced garlic, the parsley and the dill to the beaten eggs, and stir thoroughly.
   One by one, dunk the salmon filets into the wet mixture, then roll them in the crushed pistachios, coating completely.
   Place the coated salmon fillets in the Foodi SmartLid basket.
2. **Air Frying.** Close air fryer lid. Set the Foodi SmartLid timer for 10 minutes.
   When the Foodi SmartLid shuts off, after 10 minutes, the salmon will be partly cooked and the crust beginning to crisp.

Using tongs, turn each of the fish filets over.

Reset the Foodi SmartLid to 350 degrees for another 10 minutes.

After 10 minutes, when the Foodi SmartLid shuts off, the salmon will be perfectly cooked and the pistachio crust will be toasted and crispy. Using tongs, remove from the Foodi SmartLid and serve.

Louisiana Shrimp Po Boy

PREP: 10 MINUTES • COOK TIME: 10 MINUTES • TOTAL: 20 MINUTES
SERVES: 6

Ingredients
1 tsp. creole seasoning
8 slices of tomato
Lettuce leaves
¼ C. buttermilk
½ C. Louisiana Fish Fry
1 pound deveined shrimp

Remoulade sauce:
1 chopped green onion
1 tsp. hot sauce
1 tsp. Dijon mustard
½ tsp. creole seasoning
1 tsp. Worcestershire sauce
Juice of ½ a lemon
½ C. vegan mayo

Directions:
1. **Preparing the Ingredients.** To make the sauce, combine all sauce ingredients until well incorporated. Chill while you cook shrimp.
Mix seasonings together and liberally season shrimp.
Add buttermilk to a bowl. Dip each shrimp into milk and place in a Ziploc bag. Chill half an hour to marinate.
Add fish fry to a bowl. Take shrimp from marinating bag and dip into fish fry, then add to Foodi SmartLid.
Ensure your Foodi SmartLid is preheated to 400 degrees.
Spray shrimp with olive oil.
2. **Air Frying.** Close air fryer lid. Set temperature to 400°F, and set time to 5 minutes. Cook 5 minutes, flip and then cook another 5 minutes. Assemble "Keto" Po Boy by adding sauce to lettuce leaves, along with shrimp and tomato.

PER SERVING: CALORIES: 337; CARBS:5.5; FAT: 12G; PROTEIN:24G; SUGAR:2G

Old Bay Crab Cakes

PREP: 10 MINUTES • COOK TIME: 20 MINUTES • TOTAL: 30 MINUTES
SERVES: 4

Ingredients
slices dried bread, crusts removed
Small amount of milk
1 tablespoon mayonnaise
1 tablespoon Worcestershire sauce
1 tablespoon baking powder
1 tablespoon parsley flakes
1 teaspoon Old Bay® Seasoning
1/4 teaspoon salt
1 egg
1 pound lump crabmeat

Directions:

1. **Preparing the Ingredients.** Crush your bread over a large bowl until it is broken down into small pieces. Add milk and stir until bread crumbs are moistened. Mix in mayo and Worcestershire sauce. Add remaining ingredients and mix well. Shape into 4 patties.

2. **Air Frying.** Close air fryer lid. Cook at 360 degrees for 20 minutes, flip half way through.

PER SERVING: CALORIES: 165; CARBS:5.8; FAT: 4.5G; PROTEIN:24G; FIBER:0G

Scallops and Spring Veggies

PREP: 10 MINUTES • COOK TIME: 8 MINUTES • TOTAL: 18 MINUTES
SERVES: 4

Ingredients
½ pound asparagus, ends trimmed, cut into 2-inch pieces
1 cup sugar snap peas
1 pound sea scallops
1 tablespoon lemon juice
2 teaspoons olive oil
½ teaspoon dried thyme
Pinch salt
Freshly ground black pepper

Directions:
1. **Preparing the Ingredients.** Place the asparagus and sugar snap peas in the Foodi SmartLid basket.
2. **Air Frying**. Close air fryer lid. Cook for 2 to 3 minutes or until the vegetables are just starting to get tender.
   Meanwhile, check the scallops for a small muscle attached to the side, and pull it off and discard.
   In a medium bowl, toss the scallops with the lemon juice, olive oil, thyme, salt, and pepper. Place into the Foodi SmartLid basket on top of the vegetables.
3. **Air Frying**. Close air fryer lid. Steam for 5 to 7 minutes, tossing the basket once during cooking time, until the scallops are just firm when tested with your finger and are opaque in the center, and the vegetables are tender. Serve immediately.

PER SERVING: CALORIES: 162; CARBS:10G; FAT: 4G; PROTEIN:22G; FIBER:3G

Air Fryer Salmon Patties

PREP: 8 MINUTES • COOK TIME: 7 MINUTES • TOTAL: 15 MINUTES
SERVES: 4

Ingredients
1 tbsp. olive oil
1 tbsp. ghee
¼ tsp. salt
1/8 tsp. pepper
1 egg
1 C. almond flour
1 can wild Alaskan pink salmon

Directions:
1. **Preparing the Ingredients**. Drain can of salmon into a bowl and keep liquid. Discard skin and bones.
   Add salt, pepper, and egg to salmon, mixing well with hands to incorporate. Make patties.
   Dredge in flour and remaining egg. If it seems dry, spoon reserved salmon liquid from the can onto patties.
2. **Air Frying**. Add patties to the Foodi SmartLid. Close air fryer lid and cook 7 minutes at 378 degrees till golden, making sure to flip once during cooking process.

PER SERVING: CALORIES: 437; CARBS:55; FAT: 12G; PROTEIN:24G; SUGAR:2G

Salmon Noodles

PREP: 5 MINUTES • COOK TIME: 16 MINUTES • TOTAL: 21 MINUTES
SERVES: 4

Ingredients
1 Salmon Fillet
1 Tbsp Teriyaki Marinade
3 ½ Ozs Soba Noodles, cooked and drained
10 Ozs Firm Tofu
7 Ozs Mixed Salad
1 Cup Broccoli
Olive Oil
Salt and Pepper to taste

Directions:
1. **Preparing the Ingredients.** Season the salmon with salt and pepper to taste, then coat with the teriyaki marinate. Set aside for 15 minutes
2. **Air Frying.** Preheat the Foodi SmartLid at 350 degrees, close air fryer lid and cook the salmon for 8 minutes.
Whilst the Foodi SmartLid is cooking the salmon, start slicing the tofu into small cubes.
Next, slice the broccoli into smaller chunks. Drizzle with olive oil.
Once the salmon is cooked, put the broccoli and tofu into the Foodi SmartLid tray for 8 minutes.
Plate the salmon and broccoli tofu mixture over the soba noodles. Add the mixed salad to the side and serve

Beer-Battered Fish and Chips

PREP: 5 MINUTES • COOK TIME: 30 MINUTES • TOTAL: 35 MINUTES
SERVES: 4

Ingredients
2 eggs
1 cup malty beer, such as Pabst Blue Ribbon
1 cup all-purpose flour
½ cup cornstarch
1 teaspoon garlic powder
Salt
Pepper
Cooking oil
(4-ounce) cod fillets

Directions:
1. **Preparing the Ingredients.** In a medium bowl, beat the eggs with the beer. In another medium bowl, combine the flour and cornstarch, and season with the garlic powder and salt and pepper to taste.
Spray the Foodi SmartLid basket with cooking oil.
Dip each cod fillet in the flour and cornstarch mixture and then in the egg and beer mixture. Dip the cod in the flour and cornstarch a second time.
2. **Air Frying.** Place the cod in the Foodi SmartLid. Do not stack. Cook in batches. Spray with cooking oil. Close air fryer lid and cook for 8 minutes.
Open the Foodi SmartLid and flip the cod. Cook for an additional 7 minutes.
Remove the cooked cod from the Foodi SmartLid, then repeat steps 4 and 5 for the remaining fillets.
Serve with prepared air fried frozen fries. Frozen fries will need to be cooked for 18 to 20 minutes at 400ºF.
Cool before serving.

PER SERVING: CALORIES: 325; CARBS:41; FAT: 4G; PROTEIN:26G; FIBER:1G

Tuna Stuffed Potatoes

PREP: 5 MINUTES • COOK TIME: 30 MINUTES • TOTAL: 35 MINUTES
SERVES: 4

Ingredients
4 starchy potatoes
½ tablespoon olive oil
1 (6-ounce) can tuna, drained
2 tablespoons plain Greek yogurt
1 teaspoon red chili powder
Salt and freshly ground black pepper, to taste
1 scallion, chopped and divided
1 tablespoon capers

Directions:
1. **Preparing the Ingredients**. In a large bowl of water, soak the potatoes for about 30 minutes. Drain well and pat dry with paper towel.
Preheat the Foodi SmartLid to 355 degrees F. Place the potatoes in a fryer basket.
2. **Air Frying**. Close air fryer lid and cook for about 30 minutes.
Meanwhile in a bowl, add tuna, yogurt, red chili powder, salt, black pepper and half of scallion and with a potato masher, mash the mixture completely.
Remove the potatoes from the Foodi SmartLid and place onto a smooth surface. Carefully, cut each potato from top side lengthwise.
With your fingers, press the open side of potato halves slightly. Stuff the potato open portion with tuna mixture evenly.
Sprinkle with the capers and remaining scallion. Serve immediately.

Fried Calamari

PREP: 8 MINUTES • COOK TIME: 7 MINUTES • TOTAL: 15 MINUTES
SERVES: 6-8

Ingredients
½ tsp. salt
½ tsp. Old Bay seasoning
1/3 C. plain cornmeal
½ C. semolina flour
½ C. almond flour
5-6 C. olive oil
1 ½ pounds baby squid

Directions:
1. **Preparing the Ingredients.** Rinse squid in cold water and slice tentacles, keeping just ¼-inch of the hood in one piece. Combine 1-2 pinches of pepper, salt, Old Bay seasoning, cornmeal, and both flours together. Dredge squid pieces into flour mixture and place into the Foodi SmartLid.
2. **Air Frying.** Spray liberally with olive oil. Close air fryer lid and cook 15 minutes at 345 degrees till coating turns a golden brown.

PER SERVING: CALORIES: 211; CARBS:55; FAT: 6G; PROTEIN:21G; SUGAR:1G

Soy and Ginger Shrimp

PREP: 8 MINUTES • COOK TIME: 10 MINUTES • TOTAL: 15 MINUTES
SERVES: 4

Ingredients
2 tablespoons olive oil
2 tablespoons scallions, finely chopped
2 cloves garlic, chopped
1 teaspoon fresh ginger, grated
1 tablespoon dry white wine
1 tablespoon balsamic vinegar
1/4 cup soy sauce
1 tablespoon sugar
1 pound shrimp
Salt and ground black pepper, to taste

Directions:
1. **Preparing the Ingredients.** To make the marinade, warm the oil in a saucepan; cook all ingredients, except the shrimp, salt, and black pepper. Now, let it cool.
Marinate the shrimp, covered, at least an hour, in the refrigerator.
2. **Air Frying.** After that, close air fryer lid and bake the shrimp at 350 degrees F for 8 to 10 minutes (depending on the size), turning once or twice. Season prepared shrimp with salt and black pepper and serve right away!

Crispy Cheesy Fish Fingers

PREP: 10 MINUTES • COOK TIME: 20 MINUTES • TOTAL: 30 MINUTES
SERVES: 4

Ingredients
Large cod fish filet, approximately 6-8 ounces, fresh or frozen and thawed, cut into 1 ½-inch strips
2 raw eggs
½ cup of breadcrumbs (we like Panko, but any brand or home recipe will do)
2 tablespoons of shredded or powdered parmesan cheese
1 tablespoons of shredded cheddar cheese
Pinch of salt and pepper

Directions:
1. **Preparing the Ingredients.** Cover the basket of the Foodi SmartLid with a lining of tin foil, leaving the edges uncovered to allow air to circulate through the basket.
Preheat the Foodi SmartLid to 350 degrees.
In a large mixing bowl, beat the eggs until fluffy and until the yolks and whites are fully combined.
Dunk all the fish strips in the beaten eggs, fully submerging.
In a separate mixing bowl, combine the bread crumbs with the parmesan, cheddar, and salt and pepper, until evenly mixed.
One by one, coat the egg-covered fish strips in the mixed dry ingredients so that they're fully covered, and place on the foil-lined Foodi SmartLid basket.
2. **Air Frying.** Close air fryer lid. Set the air-fryer timer to 20 minutes.
Halfway through the cooking time, shake the handle of the air-fryer so that the breaded fish jostles inside and fry-coverage is even.
After 20 minutes, when the fryer shuts off, the fish strips will be perfectly cooked and their breaded crust golden-brown and delicious! Using tongs, remove from the

Foodi SmartLid and set on a serving dish to cool.

Panko-Crusted Tilapia

PREP: 5 MINUTES • COOK TIME: 10 MINUTES • TOTAL: 15 MINUTES
SERVES: 3

Ingredients
2 tsp. Italian seasoning
2 tsp. lemon pepper
1/3 C. panko breadcrumbs
1/3 C. egg whites
1/3 C. almond flour
3 tilapia fillets
Olive oil

Directions:
1. **Preparing the Ingredients.** Place panko, egg whites, and flour into separate bowls. Mix lemon pepper and Italian seasoning in with breadcrumbs.
   Pat tilapia fillets dry. Dredge in flour, then egg, then breadcrumb mixture.
2. **Air Frying.** Add to the Foodi SmartLid basket and spray lightly with olive oil. Close air fryer lid.
   Cook 10-11 minutes at 400 degrees, making sure to flip halfway through cooking.

PER SERVING: CALORIES: 256; FAT: 9G; PROTEIN:39G; SUGAR:5G

Potato Crusted Salmon

PREP: 10 MINUTES • COOK TIME: 15 MINUTES • TOTAL: 25 MINUTES
SERVES: 4

Ingredients
1 pound salmon, swordfish or arctic char fillets, 3/4 inch thick
1 egg white
2 tablespoons water
1/3 cup dry instant mashed potatoes
2 teaspoons cornstarch
1 teaspoon paprika
1 teaspoon lemon pepper seasoning

Directions:
1. **Preparing the Ingredients.** Remove and skin from the fish and cut it into 4 serving pieces Mix together the egg white and water. Mix together all of the dry ingredients. Dip the filets into the egg white mixture then press into the potato mix to coat evenly.
2. **Air Frying.** Close air fryer lid in your Foodi SmartLid, cook at 360 degrees for 15 minutes, flip the filets halfway through.

PER SERVING: CALORIES:176; FAT: 7G; PROTEIN:23G; :5G

Salmon Croquettes

PREP: 5 MINUTES • COOK TIME: 10 MINUTES • TOTAL: 15 MINUTES
SERVES: 6-8

Ingredients
Panko breadcrumbs
Almond flour
2 egg whites
2 tbsp. chopped chives
2 tbsp. minced garlic cloves
½ C. chopped onion
2/3 C. grated carrots
1 pound chopped salmon fillet

Directions:
1. **Preparing the Ingredients**. Mix together all ingredients minus breadcrumbs, flour, and egg whites.
   Shape mixture into balls. Then coat them in flour, then egg, and then breadcrumbs. Drizzle with olive oil.
2. **Air Frying.** Add coated salmon balls to Foodi SmartLid, close air fryer lid and cook 6 minutes at 350 degrees. Shake and cook an additional 4 minutes until golden in color.

PER SERVING: CALORIES: 503; CARBS:61g; FAT: 9G; PROTEIN:5G; SUGAR:4G

Snapper Scampi

PREP: 5 MINUTES • COOK TIME: 10 MINUTES • TOTAL: 15 MINUTES
SERVES: 4

Ingredients

4 (6-ounce) skinless snapper or arctic char fillets
1 tablespoon olive oil
3 tablespoons lemon juice, divided
½ teaspoon dried basil
Pinch salt
Freshly ground black pepper
2 tablespoons butter
cloves garlic, minced

Directions:
1. **Preparing the Ingredients.** Rub the fish fillets with olive oil and 1 tablespoon of the lemon juice. Sprinkle with the basil, salt, and pepper, and place in the Foodi SmartLid basket.
2. **Air Frying.** Close air fryer lid and grill the fish for 7 to 8 minutes or until the fish just flakes when tested with a fork. Remove the fish from the basket and put on a serving plate. Cover to keep warm. In a 6-by-6-by-2-inch pan, combine the butter, remaining 2 tablespoons lemon juice, and garlic. Cook in the Foodi SmartLid for 1 to 2 minutes or until the garlic is sizzling. Pour this mixture over the fish and serve.

PER SERVING: CALORIES: 265; CARBS:1g; FAT: 11G; PROTEIN:39G; FIBER:0G

Tha Fish Cakes With Mango Relish

PREP: 5 MINUTES • COOK TIME: 10 MINUTES • TOTAL: 15 MINUTES
SERVES: 4

Ingredients

1 lb White Fish Fillets
3 Tbsps Ground Coconut
1 Ripened Mango
½ Tsps Chili Paste
Tbsps Fresh Parsley
1 Green Onion
1 Lime
1 Tsp Salt
1 Egg

Directions:
1. **Preparing the Ingredients.** To make the relish, peel and dice the mango into cubes. Combine with a half teaspoon of chili paste, a tablespoon of parsley, and the zest and juice of half a lime.
   In a food processor, pulse the fish until it forms a smooth texture. Place into a bowl and add the salt, egg, chopped green onion, parsley, two tablespoons of the coconut, and the remainder of the chili paste and lime zest and juice. Combine well
   Portion the mixture into 10 equal balls and flatten them into small patties. Pour the reserved tablespoon of coconut onto a dish and roll the patties over to coat.
   Preheat the Foodi SmartLid to 390 degrees
2. **Air Frying.** Place the fish cakes into the Foodi SmartLid, close air fryer lid and cook for 8 minutes. They should be crisp and lightly browned when ready
   Serve hot with mango relish

Air Fryer Fish Tacos

PREP: 5 MINUTES • COOK TIME: 15 MINUTES • TOTAL: 20 MINUTES
SERVES: 4

Ingredients
1 pound cod
1 tbsp. cumin
½ tbsp. chili powder
1 ½ C. almond flour
1 ½ C. coconut flour
10 ounces Mexican beer
2 eggs

Directions:
1. **Preparing the Ingredients.** Whisk beer and eggs together.
   Whisk flours, pepper, salt, cumin, and chili powder together.
   Slice cod into large pieces and coat in egg mixture then flour mixture.
2. **Air Frying.** Spray bottom of your Foodi SmartLid basket with olive oil and add coated codpieces, close air fryer lid and cook 15 minutes at 375 degrees.
   Serve on lettuce leaves topped with homemade salsa.

PER SERVING: CALORIES: 178; CARBS:61g; FAT:10G; PROTEIN:19G; SUGAR:1G

Firecracker Shrimp

PREP: 10 MINUTES • COOK TIME: 8 MINUTES • TOTAL: 18 MINUTES
SERVES: 4

Ingredients
For the shrimp
1 pound raw shrimp, peeled and deveined
Salt
Pepper
1 egg
½ cup all-purpose flour
¾ cup panko bread crumbs
Cooking oil
For the firecracker sauce
⅓ cup sour cream
2 tablespoons Sriracha
¼ cup sweet chili sauce

Directions:
1. **Preparing the Ingredients.** Season the shrimp with salt and pepper to taste. In a small bowl, beat the egg. In another small bowl, place the flour. In a third small bowl, add the panko bread crumbs.
   Spray the Foodi SmartLid basket with cooking oil. Dip the shrimp in the flour, then the egg, and then the bread crumbs. Place the shrimp in the Foodi SmartLid basket. It is okay to stack them. Spray the shrimp with cooking oil.
2. **Air Frying.** Close air fryer lid and cook for 4 minutes. Open the Foodi SmartLid and flip the shrimp. I recommend flipping individually instead of shaking to keep the breading intact. Cook for an additional 4 minutes or until crisp.
   While the shrimp is cooking, make the firecracker sauce: In a small bowl, combine the sour cream, Sriracha, and sweet chili sauce. Mix well. Serve with the shrimp.

PER SERVING: CALORIES: 266; CARBS:23g; FAT:6G; PROTEIN:27G; FIBER:1G

Sesame Seeds Coated Fish

PREP: 10 MINUTES • COOK TIME: 8 MINUTES • TOTAL: 18 MINUTES
SERVES: 5

Ingredients
3 tablespoons plain flour
2 eggs
½ cup sesame seeds, toasted
½ cup breadcrumbs
1/8 teaspoon dried rosemary, crushed
Pinch of salt
Pinch of black pepper
3 tablespoons olive oil
5 frozen fish fillets (white fish of your choice)

Directions:

1. **Preparing the Ingredients.** In a shallow dish, place flour. In a second shallow dish, beat the eggs. In a third shallow dish, add remaining ingredients except fish fillets and mix till a crumbly mixture forms.
Coat the fillets with flour and shake off the excess flour.
Next, dip the fillets in egg.
Then coat the fillets with sesame seeds mixture generously.
Preheat the Foodi SmartLid to 390 degrees F.

2. **Air Frying.** Line an Foodi SmartLid basket with a piece of foil. Arrange the fillets into prepared basket. Close air fryer lid and cook for about 14 minutes, flipping once after 10 minutes.

Bacon Wrapped Scallops

PREP: 5 MINUTES • COOK TIME: 5 MINUTES • TOTAL: 10 MINUTES
SERVES: 4

Ingredients
1 tsp. paprika
1 tsp. lemon pepper
5 slices of center-cut bacon
20 raw sea scallops

Directions:
1. **Preparing the Ingredients.** Rinse and drain scallops, placing on paper towels to soak up excess moisture.
Cut slices of bacon into 4 pieces.
Wrap each scallop with a piece of bacon, using toothpicks to secure. Sprinkle wrapped scallops with paprika and lemon pepper.
2. **Air Frying.** Spray Foodi SmartLid basket with olive oil and add scallops. Close air fryer lid and cook 5-6 minutes at 400 degrees, making sure to flip halfway through.

PER SERVING: CALORIES: 389; CARBS:63g; FAT:17G; PROTEIN:21G; SUGAR:1G

Crispy Paprika Fish Fillets

PREP: 5 MINUTES • COOK TIME: 15 MINUTES • TOTAL: 20 MINUTES
SERVES: 4

Ingredients
1/2 cup seasoned breadcrumbs
1 tablespoon balsamic vinegar
1/2 teaspoon seasoned salt
1 teaspoon paprika
1/2 teaspoon ground black pepper
1 teaspoon celery seed
2 fish fillets, halved
1 egg, beaten

Directions:
1. **Preparing the Ingredients.** Add the breadcrumbs, vinegar, salt, paprika, ground black pepper, and celery seeds to your food processor. Process for about 30 seconds.
Coat the fish fillets with the beaten egg; then, coat them with the breadcrumbs mixture.
2. **Air Frying.** Close air fryer lid. Cook at 350 degrees F for about 15 minutes.

Parmesan Shrimp

PREP: 5 MINUTES • COOK TIME: 10 MINUTES • TOTAL: 15 MINUTES
SERVES: 4

Ingredients
2 tbsp. olive oil
1 tsp. onion powder
1 tsp. basil
½ tsp. oregano
1 tsp. pepper
2/3 C. grated parmesan cheese
4 minced garlic cloves
pounds of jumbo cooked shrimp (peeled/deveined)

Directions:
1. **Preparing the Ingredients**. Mix all seasonings together and gently toss shrimp with mixture.
2. **Air Frying.** Spray olive oil into the Foodi SmartLid basket and add seasoned shrimp. Close air fryer lid and cook 8-10 minutes at 350 degrees.
Squeeze lemon juice over shrimp right before devouring!

PER SERVING: CALORIES: 351; FAT:11G; PROTEIN:19G; SUGAR:1G

Flaky Fish Quesadilla

PREP: 10 MINUTES • COOK TIME: 12 MINUTES • TOTAL: 22 MINUTES
SERVES: 4

Ingredients
Two 6-inch corn or flour tortilla shells
1 medium-sized tilapia fillet, approximately 4 ounces
½ medium-sized lemon, sliced
½ an avocado, peeled, pitted and sliced
1 clove of garlic, peeled and finely minced
Pinch of salt and pepper
½ teaspoon of lemon juice
¼ cup of shredded cheddar cheese
¼ cup of shredded mozzarella cheese

Directions:
1. **Preparing the Ingredients.** Preheat the Foodi SmartLid to 350 degrees.
In the oven, grill the tilapia with a little salt and lemon slices in foil on high heat for 20 minutes.
Remove fish in foil from the oven, and break the fish meat apart into bite-sized pieces with a fork – it should be flaky and chunky when cooked.
While the fish is cooling, combine the avocado, garlic, salt, pepper, and lemon juice in a small mixing bowl; mash lightly, but don't whip - keep the avocado slightly chunky.
Spread the guacamole on one of the tortillas, then cover with the fish flakes, and then with the cheese. Top with the second tortilla.
Place directly on hot surface of the air frying basket.
2. **Air Frying.** Close air fryer lid. Set the Foodi SmartLid timer for 6 minutes.
After 6 minutes, when the Foodi SmartLid shuts off, flip the tortillas onto the other side with a spatula; the cheese should be melted enough that it won't fall apart.

Reset Foodi SmartLid to 350 degrees for another 6 minutes.

After 6 minutes, when the Foodi SmartLid shuts off, the tortillas should be browned and crisp, and the fish, guacamole and cheese will be hot and delicious inside. Remove with spatula and let sit on a serving plate to cool for a few minutes before slicing.

Quick Fried Catfish

PREP: 5 MINUTES • COOK TIME: 15 MINUTES • TOTAL: 20 MINUTES
SERVES: 4

Ingredients

3/4 cups Original Bisquick™ mix
1/2 cup yellow cornmeal
1 tablespoon seafood seasoning
4 catfish fillets (4 to 6 ounces each)
1/2 cup ranch dressing
Lemon wedges

Directions:

1 **Preparing the Ingredients.** In a shallow bowl mix together the Bisquick mix, cornmeal, and seafood seasoning. Pat the filets dry, then brush them with ranch dressing.
Press the filets into the Bisquick mix on both sides until the filet is evenly coated.
2 **Air Frying.** Close air fryer lid and cook in your Foodi SmartLid at 360 degrees for 15 minutes, flip the filets halfway through. Serve with a lemon garnish.

PER SERVING: CALORIES: 372; FAT:16G; PROTEIN:28G; FIBER:1.7G

Honey Glazed Salmon

PREP: 5 MINUTES • COOK TIME: 8 MINUTES • TOTAL: 13 MINUTES
SERVES: 2

Ingredients
1 tsp. water
3 tsp. rice wine vinegar
6 tbsp. low-sodium soy sauce
6 tbsp. raw honey
2 salmon fillets

Directions:
1. **Preparing the Ingredients.** Combine water, vinegar, honey, and soy sauce together. Pour half of this mixture into a bowl.
   Place salmon in one bowl of marinade and let chill 2 hours.
2. **Air Frying.** Ensure your Foodi SmartLid is preheated to 356 degrees and add salmon. Close air fryer lid and cook 8 minutes, flipping halfway through. Baste salmon with some of the remaining marinade mixture and cook another 5 minutes.
   To make a sauce to serve salmon with, pour remaining marinade mixture into a saucepan, heating till simmering. Let simmer 2 minutes. Serve drizzled over salmon!

PER SERVING: CALORIES: 348; FAT:12G; PROTEIN:20G; SUGAR:3G

Fish and Chips

PREP: 10 MINUTES • COOK TIME: 20 MINUTES • TOTAL: 30 MINUTES
SERVES: 4

Ingredients
4 (4-ounce) fish fillets
Pinch salt
Freshly ground black pepper
½ teaspoon dried thyme
1 egg white
¾ cup crushed potato chips
2 tablespoons olive oil, divided
3 russet potatoes, peeled and cut into strips

Directions:
1. **Preparing the Ingredients.** Pat the fish fillets dry and sprinkle with salt, pepper, and thyme. Set aside.
   In a shallow bowl, beat the egg white until foamy. In another bowl, combine the potato chips and 1 tablespoon of olive oil and mix until combined.
   Dip the fish fillets into the egg white, then into the crushed potato chip mixture to coat.
   Toss the fresh potato strips with the remaining 1 tablespoon olive oil.
2. **Air Frying.** Use your separator to divide the Foodi SmartLid basket in half, close air fryer lid and fry the chips and fish. The chips will take about 20 minutes; the fish will take about 10 to 12 minutes to cook.

PER SERVING: CALORIES: 374; FAT:16G; PROTEIN:30G; FIBER:4G

Fish Sandwiches

PREP: 10 MINUTES • COOK TIME: 20 MINUTES • TOTAL: 30 MINUTES
SERVES: 4

Ingredients
lbs White Fish Fillets
1/4 Cup Yellow Cornmeal
1 Tsp Greek Seasoning
Salt and Pepper to taste
2 ½ Cups Plain Flour
2 Tsps Baking Powder
2 Cups Beer
4 Hamburger Buns
Mayonnaise
Lettuce Leaves
1 Tomato, sliced
1 Egg

Directions:
1. **Preparing the Ingredients.** Cut the fish fillets into burger patty sized strips. Season with salt and pepper to desired taste.
   In a medium bowl, mix together the beer, egg, baking powder, plain flour, cornmeal, Greek seasoning and additional salt and pepper
   Heat the Foodi SmartLid to 340 degrees
   Place each seasoned fish strip into the batter, ensuring that it is well coated
2. **Air Frying.** Place battered fish into the Foodi SmartLid tray, close air fryer lid and cook in batches for 6 minutes or until crispy
   Compile the sandwich by topping each bun with mayonnaise, then a lettuce leaf, tomato slices, and finally the cooked fish strip

Crab Cakes

PREP: 5 MINUTES • COOK TIME: 10 MINUTES • TOTAL: 15 MINUTES
SERVES: 4

Ingredients
8 ounces jumbo lump crabmeat
1 tablespoon Old Bay Seasoning
⅓ cup bread crumbs
¼ cup diced red bell pepper
¼ cup diced green bell pepper
1 egg
¼ cup mayonnaise
Juice of ½ lemon

1 teaspoon flour
Cooking oil

Directions:
1. **Preparing the Ingredients.** In a large bowl, combine the crabmeat, Old Bay Seasoning, bread crumbs, red bell pepper, green bell pepper, egg, mayo, and lemon juice. Mix gently to combine.
   Form the mixture into 4 patties. Sprinkle ¼ teaspoon of flour on top of each patty.
2. **Air Frying.** Place the crab cakes in the Foodi SmartLid. Spray them with cooking oil. Close air fryer lid and cook for 10 minutes.
   Serve.

Crispy Air Fried Sushi Roll

PREP: 10 MINUTES • COOK TIME: 5 MINUTES • TOTAL: 15 MINUTES
SERVES: 12

Ingredients
Kale Salad:
1 tbsp. sesame seeds
¾ tsp. soy sauce
¼ tsp. ginger
1/8 tsp. garlic powder
¾ tsp. toasted sesame oil
½ tsp. rice vinegar
1 ½ C. chopped kale
Sushi Rolls:
½ of a sliced avocado
3 sheets of sushi nori
1 batch cauliflower rice
Sriracha Mayo:
Sriracha sauce
¼ C. vegan mayo
Coating:
½ C. panko breadcrumbs

Directions:
1 **Preparing the Ingredients.** Combine all of kale salad ingredients together, tossing well. Set to the side.
Lay out a sheet of nori and spread a handful of rice on. Then place 2-3 tbsp. of kale salad over rice, followed by avocado. Roll up sushi.
To make mayo, whisk mayo ingredients together until smooth.
Add breadcrumbs to a bowl.
2 **Air Frying.** Coat sushi rolls in crumbs till coated and add to the Foodi SmartLid. Close air fryer lid and cook rolls 10 minutes at 390 degrees, shaking gently at 5 minutes.
Slice each roll into 6-8 pieces and enjoy!

PER SERVING: CALORIES: 267; FAT:13G; PROTEIN:6G; SUGAR:3G

Sweet Recipes

Perfect Cinnamon Toast

PREP: 10 MINUTES • COOK TIME: 5 MINUTES • TOTAL: 15 MINUTES
SERVES: 6

Ingredients

2 tsp. pepper
1 ½ tsp. vanilla extract
1 ½ tsp. cinnamon
½ C. sweetener of choice
1 C. coconut oil
12 slices whole wheat bread

Directions:

1. **Preparing the Ingredients.** Melt coconut oil and mix with sweetener until dissolved. Mix in remaining ingredients minus bread till incorporated.
Spread mixture onto bread, covering all area.
2. **Air Frying.** Place coated pieces of bread in your Foodi SmartLid. Close air fryer lid and cook 5 minutes at 400 degrees.
Remove and cut diagonally. Enjoy!

PER SERVING: CALORIES: 124; FAT:2G; PROTEIN:0G; SUGAR:4G

Easy Baked Chocolate Mug Cake

PREP: 5 MINUTES • COOK TIME: 15 MINUTES • TOTAL: 20 MINUTES
SERVES: 3

Ingredients

½ cup cocoa powder
½ cup stevia powder
1 cup coconut cream
1 package cream cheese, room temperature
1 tablespoon vanilla extract
3 tablespoons butter

Directions:

1. **Preparing the Ingredients.** Preheat the Foodi SmartLid for 5 minutes.
In a mixing bowl, combine all ingredients. Use a hand mixer to mix everything until fluffy.
Pour into greased mugs.
Place the mugs in the fryer basket.
2. **Air Frying.** Close air fryer lid and bake for 15 minutes at 350°F.
Place in the fridge to chill before serving.

PER SERVING: CALORIES: 744; FAT:69.7G; PROTEIN:13.9G; SUGAR:4G

Angel Food Cake

PREP: 5 MINUTES • COOK TIME: 30 MINUTES • TOTAL: 35 MINUTES
SERVES: 12

Ingredients
¼ cup butter, melted
1 cup powdered erythritol
1 teaspoon strawberry extract
12 egg whites
2 teaspoons cream of tartar
A pinch of salt

Directions:
1. **Preparing the Ingredients.** Preheat the Foodi SmartLid for 5 minutes.
   Mix the egg whites and cream of tartar.
   Use a hand mixer and whisk until white and fluffy.
   Add the rest of the ingredients except for the butter and whisk for another minute.
   Pour into a baking dish.
2. **Air Frying.** Place in the Foodi SmartLid basket, close air fryer lid and cook for 30 minutes at 400°F or if a toothpick inserted in the middle comes out clean.
   Drizzle with melted butter once cooled.

PER SERVING: CALORIES: 65; FAT:5G; PROTEIN:3.1G; FIBER:1G

Fried Peaches

PREP: 2 HOURS 10 MINUTES • COOK TIME: 15 MINUTES • TOTAL: 15 MINUTES
SERVES: 4

Ingredients
4 ripe peaches (1/2 a peach = 1 serving)
1 1/2 cups flour
Salt
2 egg yolks
3/4 cups cold water
1 1/2 tablespoons olive oil
2 tablespoons brandy
4 egg whites
Cinnamon/sugar mix

Directions:
1. **Preparing the Ingredients.** Mix flour, egg yolks, and salt in a mixing bowl. Slowly mix in water, then add brandy. Set the mixture aside for 2 hours and go do something for 1 hour 45 minutes.
   Boil a large pot of water and cut and X at the bottom of each peach. While the water boils fill another large bowl with water and ice. Boil each peach for about a minute, then plunge it in the ice bath. Now the peels should basically fall off the peach. Beat the egg whites and mix into the batter mix. Dip each peach in the mix to coat.
2. **Air Frying.** Close air fryer lid and cook at 360 degrees for 10 Minutes.
   Prepare a plate with cinnamon/sugar mix, roll peaches in mix and serve.

PER SERVING: CALORIES: 306; FAT:3G; PROTEIN:10G; FIBER:2.7G

Easy Donuts

PREP: 5 MINUTES • BAKE: 5 MINUTES • PRESSURE: 5 MINUTES • TOTAL: 10 MINUTES
SERVES 8

Ingredients:
Pinch of allspice
4 tbsp. dark brown sugar
½ - 1 tsp. cinnamon
1/3 C. granulated sweetener
3 tbsp. melted coconut oil
1 can of biscuits

Directions
1. **Preparing the ingredients**. Preheat the unit by selecting Bake/Roast, setting the temperature to 300°F, and setting the time to 5 minutes. Press Start/Stop to begin.
   Mix allspice, sugar, sweetener, and cinnamon together.
   Take out biscuits from can and with a circle cookie cutter, cut holes from centers and place into Foodi SmartLid.
2. **Air Frying the Dish**. Close the air fryer Lid. Select Bake, set the temperature to 350°F, and set the time to 5 minutes. Select Start to begin. As batches are cooked, use a brush to coat with melted coconut oil and dip each into sugar mixture.
   Serve warm!

Apple Pie in Air Fryer

PREP: 5 MINUTES • COOK TIME: 35 MINUTES • TOTAL: 40 MINUTES
SERVES: 4

Ingredients
½ teaspoon vanilla extract
1 beaten egg
1 large apple, chopped
1 Pillsbury Refrigerator pie crust
1 tablespoon butter
1 tablespoon ground cinnamon
1 tablespoon raw sugar
2 tablespoon sugar
2 teaspoons lemon juice
Baking spray

Directions:
1. **Preparing the Ingredients**. Lightly grease baking pan of Foodi SmartLid with cooking spray. Spread pie crust on bottom of pan up to the sides.
   In a bowl, mix vanilla, sugar, cinnamon, lemon juice, and apples. Pour on top of pie crust. Top apples with butter slices.
   Cover apples with the other pie crust. Pierce with knife the tops of pie.
   Spread beaten egg on top of crust and sprinkle sugar.
   Cover with foil.
2. **Air Frying**. Close air fryer lid. For 25 minutes, cook on 390°F.
   Remove foil cook for 10 minutes at 330oF until tops are browned.
   Serve and enjoy.

PER SERVING: CALORIES: 372; FAT:19G; PROTEIN:4.2G; SUGAR:5G

Raspberry Cream Rol-Ups

PREP: 10 MINUTES • COOK TIME: 25 MINUTES • TOTAL: 35 MINUTES
SERVES: 4

Ingredients

1 cup of fresh raspberries, rinsed and patted dry
½ cup of cream cheese, softened to room temperature
¼ cup of brown sugar
¼ cup of sweetened condensed milk
1 egg
1 teaspoon of corn starch
6 spring roll wrappers (any brand will do, we like Blue Dragon or Tasty Joy, both available through Target or Walmart, or any large grocery chain)
¼ cup of water

Directions:

1. **Preparing the Ingredients.** Cover the basket of the Foodi SmartLid with a lining of tin foil, leaving the edges uncovered to allow air to circulate through the basket. Preheat the Foodi SmartLid to 350 degrees.

   In a mixing bowl, combine the cream cheese, brown sugar, condensed milk, cornstarch, and egg. Beat or whip thoroughly, until all ingredients are completely mixed and fluffy, thick and stiff. Spoon even amounts of the creamy filling into each spring roll wrapper, then top each dollop of filling with several raspberries.

   Roll up the wraps around the creamy raspberry filling, and seal the seams with a few dabs of water.

   Place each roll on the foil-lined Foodi SmartLid basket, seams facing down.

2. **Air Frying.** Close air fryer lid. Set the Foodi SmartLid timer to 10 minutes. During cooking, shake the handle of the fryer basket to ensure a nice even surface crisp. After 10 minutes, when the Foodi SmartLid shuts off, the spring rolls should be golden brown and perfect on the outside, while the raspberries and cream filling will have cooked together in a glorious fusion. Remove with tongs and serve hot or cold.

Air Fryer Chocolate Cake

PREP: 5 MINUTES • COOK TIME: 35 MINUTES • TOTAL: 40 MINUTES
SERVES: 8-10

Ingredients
½ C. hot water
1 tsp. vanilla
¼ C. olive oil
½ C. almond milk
1 egg
½ tsp. salt
¾ tsp. baking soda
¾ tsp. baking powder
½ C. unsweetened cocoa powder
2 C. almond flour
1 C. brown sugar

Directions:
1. **Preparing the Ingredients.** Preheat your Foodi SmartLid to 356 degrees.
Stir all dry ingredients together. Then stir in wet ingredients. Add hot water last. The batter will be thin, no worries.
2. **Air Frying.** Pour cake batter into a pan that fits into the fryer. Cover with foil and poke holes into the foil. Close the air fryer Lid. Select Bake, set the temperature to 356°F, and set the time to 35 minutes. Select Start to begin. Discard foil and then bake another 10 minutes.

PER SERVING: CALORIES: 378; FAT:9G; PROTEIN:4G; SUGAR:5G

Banana-Choco Brownies

PREP: 5 MINUTES • COOK TIME: 30 MINUTES • TOTAL: 35 MINUTES
SERVES: 12

Ingredients
2 cups almond flour
2 teaspoons baking powder
½ teaspoon baking powder
½ teaspoon baking soda
½ teaspoon salt
1 over-ripe banana
3 large eggs
½ teaspoon stevia powder
¼ cup coconut oil
1 tablespoon vinegar
1/3 cup almond flour
1/3 cup cocoa powder

Directions:
1. **Preparing the Ingredients**. Preheat the Foodi SmartLid for 5 minutes.
Combine all ingredients in a food processor and pulse until well-combined. Pour into a baking dish that will fit in the Foodi SmartLid.
2. **Air Frying.** Place in the Foodi SmartLid basket. Close the air fryer Lid. Select Bake, set the temperature to 350°F, and set the time to 30 minutes or if a toothpick inserted in the middle comes out clean. Select Start to begin.

PER SERVING: CALORIES: 75; FAT:6.5G; PROTEIN:1.7G; SUGAR:2G

Chocolate Donuts

PREP: 5 MINUTES • COOK TIME: 20 MINUTES • TOTAL: 25 MINUTES
SERVES: 8-10

Ingredients
(8-ounce) can jumbo biscuits
Cooking oil
Chocolate sauce, such as Hershey's

Directions:
1. **Preparing the Ingredients**. Separate the biscuit dough into 8 biscuits and place them on a flat work surface. Use a small circle cookie cutter or a biscuit cutter to cut a hole in the center of each biscuit. You can also cut the holes using a knife. Spray the Foodi SmartLid basket with cooking oil.
2. **Air Frying.** Place 4 donuts in the Foodi SmartLid. Do not stack. Spray with cooking oil. Close the air fryer Lid and cook for 4 minutes.
   Open the Foodi SmartLid and flip the donuts. Cook for an additional 4 minutes. Remove the cooked donuts from the Foodi SmartLid, then repeat for the remaining 4 donuts.

Drizzle chocolate sauce over the donuts and enjoy while warm.

PER SERVING: CALORIES: 181; FAT:98G; PROTEIN:3G; FIBER:1G

Easy Air fryer Donuts

PREP: 5 MINUTES • COOK TIME: 5 MINUTES • TOTAL: 10 MINUTES
SERVES: 8

Ingredients
Pinch of allspice
4 tbsp. dark brown sugar
½ - 1 tsp. cinnamon
1/3 C. granulated sweetener
3 tbsp. melted coconut oil
1 can of biscuits

Directions:
1. **Preparing the Ingredients.** Mix allspice, sugar, sweetener, and cinnamon together. Take out biscuits from can and with a circle cookie cutter, cut holes from centers and place into Foodi SmartLid.
2. **Air Frying.** Close the air fryer Lid and cook 5 minutes at 350 degrees. As batches are cooked, use a brush to coat with melted coconut oil and dip each into sugar mixture.
   Serve warm!

PER SERVING: CALORIES: 209; FAT:4G; PROTEIN:0G; SUGAR:3G

Cinnamon Rolls

PREP: 15 MINUTES • BAKE: 10 MINUTES • TOTAL: 25 MINUTES
SERVES 8

Ingredients:
1 ½ tbsp. cinnamon
¾ C. brown sugar
¼ C. melted coconut oil
1 pound frozen bread dough, thawed

Glaze:

½ tsp. vanilla
1 ¼ C. powdered erythritol
2 tbsp. softened ghee
4 ounces softened cream cheese

Directions:
1. **Preparing the ingredients**. Preheat the unit by selecting Bake, setting the temperature to 300°F, and setting the time to 5 minutes. Press Start to begin. Lay out bread dough and roll out into a rectangle. Brush melted ghee over dough and leave a 1-inch border along edges.
Mix cinnamon and sweetener together and then sprinkle over dough. Roll dough tightly and slice into 8 pieces. Let sit 1-2 hours to rise. To make the glaze, simply mix ingredients together till smooth.
2. **Finish the dish.** Once rolls rise, place into the Foodi SmartLid. Close the air fryer Lid. Select Bake, set the temperature to 350°F, and set the time to 5 minutes. Select Start to begin.
Serve rolls drizzled in cream cheese glaze. Enjoy

Fried Bananas with Chocolate Sauce

PREP: 10 MINUTES • COOK TIME: 10 MINUTES • TOTAL: 20 MINUTES
SERVES: 2

Ingredients
1 large egg
¼ cup cornstarch
¼ cup plain bread crumbs
3 bananas, halved crosswise
Cooking oil
Chocolate sauce (see Ingredient tip)

Directions:
1. **Preparing the Ingredients**. In a small bowl, beat the egg. In another bowl, place the cornstarch. Place the bread crumbs in a third bowl. Dip the bananas in the cornstarch, then the egg, and then the bread crumbs.
Spray the Foodi SmartLid basket with cooking oil. Place the bananas in the basket and spray them with cooking oil.
2. **Air Frying.** Close the air fryer Lid. Cook for 5 minutes. Open the Foodi SmartLid and flip the bananas. Cook for an additional 2 minutes. Transfer the bananas to plates.
Drizzle the chocolate sauce over the bananas, and serve.
You can make your own chocolate sauce using 2 tablespoons milk and ¼ cup chocolate chips. Heat a saucepan over medium-high heat. Add the milk and stir for 1 to 2 minutes. Add the chocolate chips. Stir for 2 minutes, or until the chocolate has melted.

PER SERVING: CALORIES: 203; FAT:6G; PROTEIN:3G; FIBER:3G

Apple Hand Pies

PREP: 5 MINUTES • COOK TIME: 8 MINUTES • TOTAL: 13 MINUTES
SERVES: 6

Ingredients
15-ounces no-sugar-added apple pie filling
1 store-bought crust

Directions:
1. **Preparing the Ingredients.** Lay out pie crust and slice into equal-sized squares. Place 2 tbsp. filling into each square and seal crust with a fork.
2. **Air Frying.** Place into the Foodi SmartLid Foodi SmartLid. Close the air fryer Lid. Select Bake, set the temperature to 390°F, and set the time to 8 minutes until golden in color. Select Start to begin.

PER SERVING: CALORIES: 278; FAT:10G; PROTEIN:5G; SUGAR:4G

Chocolaty Banana Muffins

PREP: 5 MINUTES • COOK TIME: 25 MINUTES • TOTAL: 35 MINUTES
SERVES: 12

Ingredients
¾ cup whole wheat flour
¾ cup plain flour
¼ cup cocoa powder
¼ teaspoon baking powder
1 teaspoon baking soda
¼ teaspoon salt
2 large bananas, peeled and mashed
1 cup sugar
1/3 cup canola oil
1 egg
½ teaspoon vanilla essence
1 cup mini chocolate chips

Directions:
1. **Preparing the Ingredients.** In a large bowl, mix together flour, cocoa powder, baking powder, baking soda and salt.
   In another bowl, add bananas, sugar, oil, egg and vanilla extract and beat till well combined.
   Slowly, add flour mixture in egg mixture and mix till just combined.
   Fold in chocolate chips.
   Preheat the Foodi SmartLid to 345 degrees F. Grease 12 muffin molds.
2. **Air Frying.** Transfer the mixture into prepared muffin molds evenly, close the air fryer Lid. Select Bake, set the temperature to 390°F, and set the time to 20 minutes or till a toothpick inserted in the center comes out clean. Select Start to begin. Remove the muffin molds from Foodi SmartLid and keep on wire rack to cool for about 10 minutes. Carefully turn on a wire rack to cool completely before serving.

Blueberry Lemon Muffins

PREP: 5 MINUTES • COOK TIME: 10 MINUTES • TOTAL: 15 MINUTES
SERVES: 12

Ingredients
1 tsp. vanilla
Juice and zest of 1 lemon
2 eggs
1 C. blueberries
½ C. cream
¼ C. avocado oil
½ C. monk fruit
2 ½ C. almond flour

Directions:
1. **Preparing the Ingredients**. Mix monk fruit and flour together.
   In another bowl, mix vanilla, egg, lemon juice, and cream together. Add mixtures together and blend well.
   Spoon batter into cupcake holders.
2. **Air Frying**. Place in Foodi SmartLid. Close the air fryer Lid. Select Bake, set the temperature to 320°F, and set the time to 10 minutes. Select Start to begin checking at 6 minutes to ensure you don't overbake them.

PER SERVING: CALORIES: 317; FAT:11G; PROTEIN:3G; SUGAR:5G

Sweet Cream Cheese Wontons

PREP: 5 MINUTES • COOK TIME: 5 MINUTES • TOTAL: 10 MINUTES
SERVES: 16

Ingredients
1 egg mixed with a bit of water
Wonton wrappers
½ C. powdered erythritol
8 ounces softened cream cheese
Olive oil

Directions:
1. **Preparing the Ingredients**.
   Mix sweetener and cream cheese together. Lay out 4 wontons at a time and cover with a dish towel to prevent drying out.
   Place ½ of a teaspoon of cream cheese mixture into each wrapper.
   Dip finger into egg/water mixture and fold diagonally to form a triangle. Seal edges well.
   Repeat with remaining ingredients.
2. **Air Frying.** Place filled wontons into the Foodi SmartLid. Close the air fryer Lid. Select Bake and cook 5 minutes at 400 degrees, shaking halfway through cooking.

PER SERVING: CALORIES: 303; FAT:3G; PROTEIN:0.5G; SUGAR:4G

Air Fryer Cinnamon Rolls

PREP: 15 MINUTES • COOK TIME: 5 MINUTES • TOTAL: 15 MINUTES
SERVES: 8

Ingredients
1 ½ tbsp. cinnamon
¾ C. brown sugar
¼ C. melted coconut oil
1 pound frozen bread dough, thawed
Glaze:
½ tsp. vanilla
1 ¼ C. powdered erythritol
2 tbsp. softened ghee
3 ounces softened cream cheese

Directions:
1. **Preparing the Ingredients.** Lay out bread dough and roll out into a rectangle. Brush melted ghee over dough and leave a 1-inch border along edges.
Mix cinnamon and sweetener together and then sprinkle over dough.
Roll dough tightly and slice into 8 pieces.
Let sit 1-2 hours to rise.
To make the glaze, simply mix ingredients together till smooth.
2. **Air Frying.** Once rolls rise, place into Foodi SmartLid. Close the air fryer Lid. Select Bake and cook 5 minutes at 350 degrees.
Serve rolls drizzled in cream cheese glaze. Enjoy!

PER SERVING: CALORIES: 390; FAT:8G; PROTEIN:1G; SUGAR:7G

Bread Pudding with Cranberry

PREP: 5 MINUTES • COOK TIME: 45 MINUTES • TOTAL: 50 MINUTES
SERVES: 4

Ingredients
1-1/2 cups milk
2-1/2 eggs
1/2 cup cranberries1 teaspoon butter
1/4 cup and 2 tablespoons white sugar
1/4 cup golden raisins
1/8 teaspoon ground cinnamon
3/4 cup heavy whipping cream
3/4 teaspoon lemon zest
3/4 teaspoon kosher salt
3/4 French baguettes, cut into 2-inch slices
3/8 vanilla bean, split and seeds scraped away

Directions:
1. **Preparing the Ingredients.** Lightly grease baking pan of Foodi SmartLid with cooking spray. Spread baguette slices, cranberries, and raisins.
In blender, blend well vanilla bean, cinnamon, salt, lemon zest, eggs, sugar, and cream. Pour over baguette slices. Let it soak for an hour.
Cover pan with foil.
2. **Air Frying.** close the air fryer Lid. Select Bake and cook for 35 minutes, cook on 330°F.
Let it rest for 10 minutes.
Serve and enjoy.

PER SERVING: CALORIES: 581; FAT:23.8G; PROTEIN:15.8G; SUGAR:7G

Black and White Brownies

PREP: 10 MINUTES • COOK TIME: 20 MINUTES • TOTAL: 30 MINUTES
SERVES: 8

Ingredients
1 egg
¼ cup brown sugar
2 tablespoons white sugar
2 tablespoons safflower oil
1 teaspoon vanilla
¼ cup cocoa powder
⅓ cup all-purpose flour
¼ cup white chocolate chips
Nonstick baking spray with flour

Directions:
1. **Preparing the Ingredients.** In a medium bowl, beat the egg with the brown sugar and white sugar. Beat in the oil and vanilla. Add the cocoa powder and flour, and stir just until combined. Fold in the white chocolate chips.
Spray a 6-by-6-by-2-inch baking pan with nonstick spray. Spoon the brownie batter into the pan.
2. **Air Frying.** Close the air fryer Lid. Select Bake, and bake for 20 minutes or until the brownies are set when lightly touched with a finger. Let cool for 30 minutes before slicing to serve.

PER SERVING: CALORIES: 81; FAT:4G; PROTEIN:1G; FIBER:1G

French Toast Bites

PREP: 5 MINUTES • COOK TIME: 15 MINUTES • TOTAL: 20 MINUTES
SERVES: 8

Ingredients
Almond milk
Cinnamon
Sweetener
3 eggs
4 pieces wheat bread

Directions:
1. **Preparing the Ingredients.** Preheat the Foodi SmartLid to 360 degrees.
Whisk eggs and thin out with almond milk.
Mix 1/3 cup of sweetener with lots of cinnamon.
Tear bread in half, ball up pieces and press together to form a ball.
Soak bread balls in egg and then roll into cinnamon sugar, making sure to thoroughly coat.
2. **Air Frying.** Place coated bread balls into the Foodi SmartLid, close the air fryer Lid. Select Bake, and bake 15 minutes.

PER SERVING: CALORIES: 289; FAT:11G; PROTEIN:0G; SUGAR:4G

Baked Apple

PREP: 5 MINUTES • COOK TIME: 20 MINUTES • TOTAL: 25 MINUTES
SERVES: 4

Ingredients
¼ C. water
¼ tsp. nutmeg
¼ tsp. cinnamon
1 ½ tsp. melted ghee
2 tbsp. raisins
2 tbsp. chopped walnuts
1 medium apple

Directions:
1. **Preparing the Ingredients.** Preheat your Foodi SmartLid to 350 degrees.
   Slice apple in half and discard some of the flesh from the center.
   Place into frying pan.
   Mix remaining ingredients together except water. Spoon mixture to the middle of apple halves.
   Pour water over filled apples.
2. **Air Frying.** Place pan with apple halves into the Foodi SmartLid, close the air fryer Lid. Select Bake, bake 20 minutes.

PER SERVING: CALORIES: 199; FAT:9G; PROTEIN:1G; SUGAR:3G

Coffee And Blueberry Cake

PREP: 5 MINUTES • COOK TIME: 35 MINUTES • TOTAL: 40 MINUTES
SERVES: 6

Ingredients
1 cup white sugar
1 egg
1/2 cup butter, softened
1/2 cup fresh or frozen blueberries
1/2 cup sour cream
1/2 teaspoon baking powder
1/2 teaspoon ground cinnamon
1/2 teaspoon vanilla extract
1/4 cup brown sugar
1/4 cup chopped pecans
1/8 teaspoon salt
1-1/2 teaspoons confectioners' sugar for dusting
3/4 cup and 1 tablespoon all-purpose flour

Directions:
1. **Preparing the Ingredients.** In a small bowl, whisk well pecans, cinnamon, and brown sugar.
   In a blender, blend well all wet Ingredients. Add dry Ingredients except for confectioner's sugar and blueberries. Blend well until smooth and creamy.
   Lightly grease baking pan of Foodi SmartLid with cooking spray.
   Pour half of batter in pan. Sprinkle half of pecan mixture on top. Pour the remaining batter. And then topped with remaining pecan mixture.
   Cover pan with foil.
2. **Air Frying.** Close the air fryer Lid. Select Bake, and cook for 35 minutes, on 330°F.
   Serve and enjoy with a dusting of confectioner's sugar.

PER SERVING: CALORIES: 471; FAT:24G; PROTEIN:4.1G; SUGAR:6G

Cinnamon Sugar Roasted Chickpeas

PREP: 5 MINUTES • COOK TIME: 10 MINUTES • TOTAL: 15 MINUTES
SERVES: 2

Ingredients
1 tbsp. sweetener
1 tbsp. cinnamon
1 C. chickpeas

Directions:
1. **Preparing the Ingredients.** Preheat Foodi SmartLid to 390 degrees.
   Rinse and drain chickpeas.
   Mix all ingredients together and add to Foodi SmartLid.
2. **Air Frying.** close the air fryer Lid. Select Bake, Cook 10 minutes.

PER SERVING: CALORIES: 111; FAT:19G; PROTEIN:16G; SUGAR:5G

Cherry-Choco Bars

PREP: 5 MINUTES • COOK TIME: 15 MINUTES • TOTAL: 20 MINUTES
SERVES: 8

Ingredients
¼ teaspoon salt
½ cup almonds, sliced
½ cup chia seeds
½ cup dark chocolate, chopped
½ cup dried cherries, chopped
½ cup prunes, pureed
½ cup quinoa, cooked
¾ cup almond butter
1/3 cup honey
2 cups old-fashioned oats
2 tablespoon coconut oil

Directions:
1. **Preparing the Ingredients.** Preheat the Foodi SmartLid to 375°F.
   In a mixing bowl, combine the oats, quinoa, chia seeds, almond, cherries, and chocolate.
   In a saucepan, heat the almond butter, honey, and coconut oil.
   Pour the butter mixture over the dry mixture. Add salt and prunes.
   Mix until well combined.
   Pour over a baking dish that can fit inside the Foodi SmartLid.
2. **Air Frying.** Close the air fryer Lid. Select Bake, Cook for 15 minutes at 375°F.
   Let it cool for an hour before slicing into bars.

PER SERVING: CALORIES: 321; FAT:17G; PROTEIN:7G; SUGAR:5G

Cinnamon Fried Bananas

PREP: 5 MINUTES • COOK TIME: 10 MINUTES • TOTAL: 15 MINUTES
SERVES: 2-3

Ingredients
1 C. panko breadcrumbs
3 tbsp. cinnamon
½ C. almond flour
3 egg whites
8 ripe bananas
3 tbsp. vegan coconut oil

Directions:
1. **Preparing the Ingredients.** Heat coconut oil and add breadcrumbs. Mix around 2-3 minutes until golden. Pour into bowl.
Peel and cut bananas in half. Roll each bananas half into flour, eggs, and crumb mixture.
2. **Air Frying.** Place into the Foodi SmartLid. Close the air fryer Lid. Select Bake, and cook 10 minutes at 280 degrees.
A great addition to a healthy banana split!

PER SERVING: CALORIES: 219; FAT:10G; PROTEIN:3G; SUGAR:5G

Coconutty Lemon Bars

PREP: 5 MINUTES • COOK TIME: 25 MINUTES • TOTAL: 30 MINUTES
SERVES: 12

Ingredients
¼ cup cashew
¼ cup fresh lemon juice, freshly squeezed
¾ cup coconut milk
¾ cup erythritol
1 cup desiccated coconut
1 teaspoon baking powder
2 eggs, beaten
2 tablespoons coconut oil
A Foodi SmartLid of salt

Directions:
1. **Preparing the Ingredients.** Preheat the Foodi SmartLid for 5 minutes. In a mixing bowl, combine all ingredients. Use a hand mixer to mix everything. Pour into a baking dish that will fit in the Foodi SmartLid.
2. **Air Frying.** Close the air fryer Lid. Select Bake and cook for 25 minutes at 350°F or until a toothpick inserted in the middle comes out clean.

PER SERVING: CALORIES: 118; FAT:10G; PROTEIN:2.6G; SUGAR:5G

Conclusions

I am also thankful to the cooks who have evaluated all these recipes. You're, as well as the comments that came from your family members and friends, were invaluable.

If you have the time and inclination, please consider leaving a short review wherever you can, we would love to learn more about your opinion.

https://www.amazon.com/review/review-your-purchases/

About the Author

Linda is a New York-based food writer, an experienced chef. She loves sharing Easy, Delicious, and Healthy recipes, especially the delicious and healthy meals that can be prepared using her Foodi SmartLid-Pot. When she's not cooking, Linda enjoys spending time with her husband and her kids, chasing her 2-year-old Yorkshire terrier, gardening, and traveling.

Printed in Great Britain
by Amazon